FACT:

November 2007: Amazon lau[...]

One week later: Stephen Windwalker releases his first Kindle user's guide. It spends 17 weeks as the #1 bestselling title in Amazon's Kindle Store.

October 2008: Oprah Winfrey spends an entire program endorsing the Kindle, which had sold a little over half a million units up until then. The Kindle sells out less than 10 days later and remains sold out until February.

February 2009: Amazon launches Kindle 2, followed soon by the DX and Kindle for iPhone App.

September 2009: In the clearest signal yet of the coming ebook revolution, Kindle downloads of Dan Brown's *The Lost Symbol* outpace Amazon hardcover sales on the bestseller's release date.

December 2013: According to projections by analysts at *Tech-On*, one of Asia's most popular websites, the worldwide number of Kindles and other ebook readers will reach 28.6 million.

Today: On this day in 2009 or 2010, as you read these first pages of *The Complete User's Guide to the Amazing Amazon Kindle 2*, you are about to take your rightful place as a citizen of Kindle Nation and an active, informed participant in The Kindle Revolution.

The Complete User's Guide
To the Amazing Amazon Kindle 2

Tips, Tricks, & Links to Unlock Cool Features & Save
You Hundreds on Kindle Content

(Newly Revised - September 2009)

By Stephen Windwalker of *Kindle Nation Daily*
*The World's Leading Author on the Kindle
And How to Get the Most Out of It*

KINDLE NATION DAILY

AN IMPRINT OF HARVARD PERSPECTIVES PRESS

The Complete User's Guide to the Amazing Amazon Kindle
2: Tips, Tricks, & Links to Unlock Cool Features & Save You
Hundreds on Kindle Content
By Stephen Windwalker

1st Edition - September 2009 - ISBN 1440471584

Kindle Nation Daily, an imprint of Harvard Perspectives
Press
kindlenation@gmail.com
Arlington, Massachusetts
http://thekindlenationblog.blogspot.com/

Unattributed quotations are by Stephen Windwalker.

Acknowledgments

My heartfelt appreciation to so many, including:

*My sister Deborah, my friends Rena, Paul, Larry, Janie,
Stewart, Ned, Steve, Nick, Betty, René, Ariane, Bill, Pete,
Annie, and my three wonderful children Moriah, Adrienne
and Danny, for belief, encouragement, enthusiasm, and more*

*Thousands of helpful readers of my first Kindle guide, whose
questions, ideas, and comments have helped make this a better
book*

*Adrienne Cousins for a terrific job in enriching the resources
I am able to offer to Kindle owners in this book*

*And Manuel Burgos at RareArts Communications for being
steadfast and gifted in his commitment to help me present the
paperback editions of my books in appealing packages*

It's a sort of electronic book....

From my Kindle's "My Clippings" text file, a little passage I noticed while reading aloud to my son....

========== **The Hitchhiker's Guide to the Galaxy** (Douglas Adams) - Highlight Loc. 734-48 | Added on Saturday, September 12, 2009, 08:33 AM

"What is it?" asked Arthur.

"The Hitchhiker's Guide to the Galaxy. It's a sort of electronic book...."

Arthur turned it over nervously in his hands. "I like the cover," he said....

"I'll show you how it works," said Ford. He snatched it from Arthur, who was still holding it as if it were a two-week-dead lark, and pulled it out of its cover. "You press this button here, you see, and the screen lights up, giving you the index."

A screen, about three inches by four, lit up and characters began to flicker across the surface.

"You want to know about Vogons, so I entered that name so." His fingers tapped some more keys....

The words Vogon Constructor Fleets flared in green across the screen. Ford pressed a large red button at the bottom of the screen and words began to undulate across it. At the same time, the book began to speak the entry as well in a still, quiet, measured voice. ==========

Douglas Adams' novel *The Hitchhiker's Guide to the Galaxy*, Copyright 1979 by Serious Productions Ltd., is available on your Kindle, of course.

The Complete User's Guide to the Amazing Amazon Kindle 2

TABLE OF CONTENTS

Introduction

1. How to Use This Book

Welcome to the world of the amazing Amazon Kindle 2.

If you've just purchased and received your Kindle 2, you are in for a treat – a whole new world of reading, and an astonishing array of other features that you may not have expected.

My primary purpose here is to help you get the most out of your Kindle 2. With that in mind, let me introduce myself. While most books that are aimed at helping people use technology have been written by tech-savvy gadget heads who could probably write entire books in some sort of mysterious HTQRSXYZML code, this one is different. Like the subject of the amusing P.O.E.M. commercial parodies on Garrison Keillor's weekly radio program, I am, or was, an English major. I am also a lifelong reader with decades of experience in the fields of publishing, editing, bookselling, and occasionally literate journalism. I've written several books and articles including a very successful book about b.k. Amazon (yes, there was an Amazon *before* the *Kindle*) and how it conducts its business, but my first passion as a reader and an author has always been fiction and narrative nonfiction. I believe that most of the people who will lay out $299 to buy a Kindle 2 from here on out are likely to be serious readers first and foremost, and thus, whether they are students, retirees, or somewhere in between, kindred spirits. I hope that the way I have approached this book will be a good fit for you. I'm writing for human beings, not gadget heads.

You may want to pace yourself and balance the process of getting to know your Kindle 2 as you work your way through the book. Read a section, try it out, read some more, and so forth.

This may be counter-intuitive, but if you'd like to be able to follow along in this text while you try things out and get to know your Kindle, you may find it convenient to have a paperback version of the text, or to be able to navigate to some of its links on your computer. I've tried to make this easy to accomplish. If you are reading this on your Kindle, you can get an inexpensive companion paperback edition of this book easily in Amazon's main store by clicking on the link at my "A Kindle Home Page" website. On that same Kindle Home Page website, you'll find a complete set of the links contained in this book so that you can access them from your computer or even reorganize and customize sublists of them to send to your Kindle. (And, as we'll discuss below, you may also want to visit the Kindle Nation Daily blog. You can sign up in the Kindle Store to have each post pushed to your Kindle in real time for a total expenditure of just 99 cents a month, to keep up with the daily tips, tricks, and offers of free Kindle content that we share there.)

This is a book not only for owners of the Amazon Kindle 2, but also for others who are considering the purchase of a Kindle 2. The next section of this introduction is intended to help you determine whether a Kindle 2 or one of the other models makes the most sense for you. And if you already own a first-generation Kindle or even a Kindle DX, you may want to use this guide to decide whether an upgrade to the Kindle 2 is worth your while. If so, you will even find a chapter whose aim is to help you to sell or donate your venerable old Kindle 1 so that an upgrade might make better economic sense. You can probably defray about half the cost of a Kindle 2, or a third of the cost of a Kindle DX, by selling your Kindle 1, if you choose to do so.

If you've been reading books for years but you just got your Kindle 2, you are, as I said above, in for a treat. My own experiences with the Kindle over the past two years have convinced me that it delivers well on Amazon CEO Jeff Bezos' goal of making the device and everything else dissolve and disappear so that your reading experience is just you and the author's words.

But I also want to speak the heresy that there are certain Kindle features that change the process of reading *for the better*. The Kindle 2 technology can actually improve upon the experience of reading a physical book. One of these that I want to mention right away involves the notion of an "index," and the ways in which Kindle owners are able to search internally within whatever they are reading. For example, the traditional book convention of an index makes no particular sense in a Kindle document.

First, of course, there are no page numbers in a Kindle edition, for the simple reason that you as a reader control the size of the text font that you are reading, and therefore the number of words on a page. (The Kindle uses "locations" instead of "page numbers," which takes a little getting used to). Second, why use an index when you can type in any word or phrase with the Kindle keyboard and the Kindle will automatically display a screen that allows you to choose among the options of searching the document you are reading, your onboard dictionary, other items on your Kindle, any document in the Kindle Store, Wikipedia, or Google?

I am sure that I am not the only one, after months of reading on a Kindle, who has found myself tapping my fingertip on a word in a physical book or periodical in some sort of lapse driven by muscle memory into a magical belief that the tapping might bring up a definition, a Wikipedia listing, or an associated website.

You can add value to your purchase of this book in other ways: if you sign up for the free weekly Kindle Nation email newsletter or subscribe to have the same posts delivered daily in real-time to your Kindle, you will receive useful updates, notifications of free Kindle books or other free content in the Kindle Store or elsewhere, and additrional tips and tactics for getting the most out of your Kindle. The Kindle Nation newsletter comes out each Tuesday in a simple, brief, email-friendly format, because we don't want to keep you from the other reading for which you bought your Kindle in the first place.

If you are looking for a similarly comprehensive guide for the first-generation Kindle, check out my book *The Complete User's Guide to the Amazing Amazon Kindle 1*, which is also available both as a Kindle edition and in a popular paperback version that was published by Harvard Perspectives Press in August 2008. I am happy to report that this guide was by far the most popular guide for the first-generation Kindle, spending 17 weeks as the number one selling title of any genre in the Kindle Store and selling more copies than all other Kindle guides combined.

As you are probably aware, Amazon also provides several useful documents to support the Kindle. These include a basic Kindle User's Guide that you will find on your Kindle Home screen when you power up the Kindle for the first time, and a License Agreement with terms and conditions that can also be viewed on Amazon's website.

Please be sure to read these documents from Amazon and make appropriate use of Amazon's Kindle Support program. This book is intended to supplement the information provided in the materials that you receive from Amazon, not to replace it. I understand that you are eager to begin reading other content on your Kindle, but the little bit of time that you will spend learning to navigate the device is bound to pay off during the years of enjoyment you will get from your new Kindle. Thus I am purposely keeping the "out-of-the-box" start-up content in this book to a minimum, and placing it later in the book than would be the case if you did not have the benefit of the official Amazon documentation.

*   *   *

Although I've taken pains to include a live, interactive, hyper-linked Table of Contents as well as a wide selection of useful external web links in the *electronic* version of this book, I am sure there will be many readers who will not have direct access to these active hyperlinks, including readers of this paperback edition (no matter how hard you may tap on the links with your finger!) and readers who find this book in another electronic format through the Smashwords digital edition. There will also be Kindle edition readers who will want to access these links on their computer rather than on a Kindle. In order to provide a useful work-around for you, if you are one of these readers, I decided to make a free listing of all of these links available at my "A Kindle Home Page" website. I hope this is helpful, and I hope you agree that it is preferable to the alternative of cluttering this text with long URLs that many readers would then have to type manually into their web browsers. For readers who have trouble with the Table of Contents hyperlinks here due to the limitations of the platform on which you may be reading, my best suggestion is that you try typing in a short phrase from any Table of Contents line and let your device's search features help you find what you are seeking.

*   *   *

In various chapters of this book, I provide very specific instructions, screenshots, and similar material to help you use specific Kindle features as well as external websites and services such as Calibre or Instapaper. The hazard that accompanies such offerings, especially with applications that are in "beta" mode (as is the case with Calibre at this writing), is that little tweaks and updates along the way may render my screenshots, steps, or other material slightly dated either at the time you purchase this book or later. It's the nature of the beast when one writes about new services and sites, of course, but to the extent possible I will try to provide updated material at A Kindle Home Page.

*   *   *

Given the myriad ways in which Kindle owners are using their Kindles, there is a certain organizational challenge in trying to bring order to a project such as this book. If you think that I have left out something important and potentially useful, I hope that you will consider dropping me an email at KindleNation@gmail.com. Let me know your thoughts, and I will make every effort to be responsive, both specifically to you and more publicly in a future edition of this book.

I know that many people who are beginning to use a Kindle 2 now were among the early adopters who began Kindling with the original Kindle device. On the off chance that you are one of these people and you are seeking to dispose of the Kindle 1, I'm including a brief chapter with some suggestions for how you might proceed. But first, just in case you're still in the process of deciding, let's take a brief look at the question of which Kindle, if any, is right for you.

2. Which Kindle is Right for You?

If you're still in the process of making a Kindle purchase decision, here are a few things to keep in mind. Each of the three Kindles that are on the market as of September 2009 has its own pros and cons, and how you evaluate them will depend mightily on your own personal preferences, idiosyncracies, and reading practices.

The **Kindle 1**, which was launched on November 19, 2007 and ceased production late in 2008, is still available in two ways from Amazon. First, you can get a refurbished Kindle 1 model in as-new condition for $149 from Amazon's Warehouse Deals store. Second, you can go to Amazon Marketplace, a store for third-party sellers on the Amazon website, and buy a Kindle 1 from its current owner for a price in the $125 to $225 range.

The **Kindle 1** weighs about the same – just over 10 ounces – as the Kindle 2. It has less storage space, less speaker volume, less "cursor" mobility, shorter battery life, less powerful wireless, and less warranty protection than the Kindle 2, but it does have three strong selling points in a head-to-head comparison with its successor model:

* It is cheaper by over one-third.

* It is seen by many Kindle owners as having better display contrast than the Kindle 2.

* It has supplemental storage capacity in the form of an SD memory card slot, where you can place an SD card with memory ranging from 2 gigabytes to 8 gigabytes to maintain thousands more books and other files in easily accessible, fully integrated Kindle 1 storage.

The **Kindle DX** is the pricey youngest member of the Kindle family, currently at $489 but likely to come down in price or the 2009 holiday season. Once you recover from sticker shock, there is an awful lot to like about the DX, and the main selling point is that its 9.7-inch display (on the diagonal, of course) allows for beautiful large-sized fonts and a "page to page" reading experience that comes much closer to that of a full-sized book than one finds with the Kindle 1, the Kindle 2, or any other e-reader. You can buy it new in the Kindle Store with full warranty protection, and it comes with greater storage, more powerful wireless, a more readable display, more powerful speakers, and longer battery life than either the Kindle 1 or the Kindle 2. With the large display and its native ability to read your own PDF files without any need to send them to Amazon for conversion, the Kindle DX has been marketed by Amazon both as a replacement for backpacks full of heavy school and college textbooks and as a savior for the newspaper industry.

All that being said, the Kindle DX still has its detractors even beyond the issue of its price. Among customer gripes about the DX:

> * It weighs twice as much as the Kindle 1 or Kindle 2, does not fit neatly into the same range of compact carrying bags that can accommodate the first two Kindles, and is a bit cumbersome for one-handed reading for just about anyone who doesn't work out with weights on a regular basis.

> * Its native PDF reader is vastly limited by the fact that it has no pan or zoom features, and falls short of satisfactory viewing experience whenever the material to be viewed is too small (or large) to fit the DX screen nicely.

> * Its keyboard is actually a step backward from the Kindle 2 keyboard, since despite there being more available space the DX has no number row, forcing users to hold down the ALT key while typing in top-row letters if they want to "go to" a Kindle document location.

Still, you may well find the Kindle DX to be a terrific device if you intend to use it for charts, tables, textbooks, cookbooks, periodical graphics, web browsing and similar purposes where the large display screen will come in handy. As more and more people and organizations become familiar with the DX and its features, it is proving useful in a variety of professional applications from flight control to meeting musicians' sheet music needs.

This book, of course, is all about the Kindle 2, and reading through it should give you a very good idea of whether the Kindle in the middle is the right Kindle for you. Sales of the Kindle 2 have been exceptionally strong since Amazon lowered its price to $299 (and just $219 for "as new" refurbished Kindle 2s). If most of your reading is in book form and is light on graphics, charts, tables and the like, the Kindle 2 may be ideal for you.

One drawback that may have kept some people from buying a Kindle is that, at present, it is not available in any stores other than

Amazon's on-line store. However, Amazon's chief of Kindle operations, Ian Freed, has actually come out and encouraged people to use Amazon's liberal, hassle-free 30-day-return policy to test-drive either the Kindle 2 or the Kindle DX. You have to put the money up in advance, of course, and you only get it back if you return the Kindle for a refund, but otherwise it's a simple proposition. Just go to the Kindle Store and buy either model, try it out for (a little less than) 30 days, and if you don't like it, return it hassle-free for a full refund. All you'll be out, in the long run, is whatever you paid for Kindle content.

One last route that you may wish to try is the "No Kindle Required" approach. Since Amazon's real agenda with the Kindle is to sell Kindle content, it is happily allowing the creation of "Kindle Apps" for other devices. The process began with the iPhone and iPod Touch early in 2009, and will likely spread to the Blackberry, other mobile devices, and netbooks in the next few years. If you already have an iPhone or iPod Touch, you will definitely want to download the Kindle for Iphone app free from the iTunes Apps Store, and then spend 99 cents for a copy of my guide, No Kindle Required: The Complete Kindle for iPhone User's Guide. If you don't own a Kindle yet, your iPhone or iPod Touch can be your introduction to ebooks. If you have a Kindle, your i-device will synch up perfectly with the Kindle so that even when you leave the Kindle home you can read a few pages of your current favorite book in almost any circumstance.

3. Several Options for Disposing of Your Kindle 1

There will be a great many Kindle 1 owners who stick with their first-generation Kindles for years, and I don't blame them a bit. The original Kindle provides a great reading experience.

However, if you are one of those people who are transitioning from a Kindle 1 to a Kindle 2 or Kindle DX, here are a few suggestions for what to do with your Kindle 1. Change is seldom easy, but with a little imagination you can make a relatively painless transition from your first-generation Kindle to the Kindle 2. I certainly understand that the expense of the Kindle – the money that you spent on the original Kindle and the amount that you may spend on a Kindle 2 – is a serious consideration, especially in the current economic circumstances that many of us face.

Chances are that you spent either $359 or $399 on a Kindle 1 if you bought it new between November 2007 and November 2008, although you may have spent as much as $1,000 or more if you bought your Kindle on eBay during one of Amazon's lengthy Kindle shipping delays, or as little as $259 or $309 if you took advantage of promotions involving Oprah Winfrey or Chase Visa. Amazon no longer sells the Kindle 1 as a new device, but "as new" refurbished Kindles are currently available for under $150 in Amazon's Warehouse Deals store. Whatever the amount that you may have spent on your first Kindle, you may want to recoup some of that original expenditure if you are going to turn around and spend another $299 for the Kindle 2 or $489 for a Kindle DX.

First, give serious thought to the idea of keeping it close to home for use by your partner, a child, a parent, or a friend. You may even want to keep it as a backup. While this will not recover any money, it may save money in the long run through savings on books and other content, by supplanting a family member's potential expense for high-priced data connectivity with some other device, or by making it "unnecessary" for your household to purchase yet another Kindle.

If you plan to use the original Kindle in association with the same account that is tied to your new Kindle 2, you will be able to share books and other documents and even synchronize "last page read" between Kindles using WhisperSync. However, if two people on the same account are reading the same book on synchronized Kindles, you will want to turn WhisperSync off on the Manage Your Kindle page of your Amazon account, so that the two of you don't drive each other nuts losing each other's place! (You can also disable the feature by which Amazon backs up your Kindle content annotations, highlights, and bookmarks, if you are concerned that it may infringe on your privacy either with Amazon or with other Kindle users on your Amazon account. Just press Home, then press Menu, select "Settings" with the 5-way controller," press Menu again, and select "Disable Annotations Backup," which is a "toggle" setting).

Second, if you don't wish to keep your Kindle 1 for yourself or someone close to you, you may want to consider donating your old Kindle to a library, school, or other tax-deductible organization or agency. While this won't put cold hard cash directly and immediately into your pocket, it may provide you with a significant income-tax deduction and it could also provide you with the very rewarding feeling that you passed your Kindle on to a place where it could make a difference in the lives, education, or cultural experience of others. More and more libraries and educational institutions are acquiring Kindles for their patrons, students, and faculty. The local library in my neighboring town of Belmont recently received a gift of 10 Kindles from philanthropists Liz and Graham Allison, and even if you only have one Kindle to donate, I'm sure that there are institutions in your community that could put such a gift to good use and provide you with documentation for tax purposes.

Finally, if you do wish to sell your first-generation Kindle, you will find a fairly brisk "Kindle 1" aftermarket on eBay and in the Amazon Marketplace. Generally my recommendation here is that you use eBay only if your have prior experience selling items on eBay and no experience with Amazon Marketplace. You can also bring your Kindle in to an eBay drop-off center – they operate under a variety of different names in communities across the country – if you prefer to avoid the transaction, shipping, and service obligations.

Otherwise, it makes more sense to sell your old Kindle via Amazon Marketplace, where there is a little less of a Wild West atmosphere and a more consistent price range than you will probably find at eBay. The market price seems to have settled between $129 and $229, at this writing, for buying and selling used first-generation Kindles in "very good" or "like new" condition. You will be able to list your Kindle for sale right on the same Amazon product detail page that Amazon used to sell the original Kindle. The fact that this market has held suggests that significant numbers of people are opting to buy the Kindle 1 at what amounts to a discount of over 50 per cent off its previous retail price.

Listing your Kindle on Amazon Marketplace isn't rocket science. Check out the other listings to see the kinds of things that other sellers find it important to say in their descriptions. Be sure to describe the Kindle accurately and disclose any and all flaws. Deregister your Kindle (on your Amazon account's "Manage Your Kindle" page) before you ship it, and use your USB connection with your computer's "Finder" or "My Computer" feature to delete your files and personal documents from your Kindle. Ship the Kindle securely and promptly and make sure you pay for insurance and delivery confirmation. If you really want to school yourself on Amazon Marketplace before you list your Kindle for sale, well, I would be remiss not to recommend that you read my 2002 book Selling Used Books Online which is available for just 99 cents in a Kindle edition. Not only could the detailed information on how to make the most of your experience with Amazon Marketplace help you with the process of selling a first-generation Kindle, but it could also prove beneficial if your Kindle experience has led you to decide to downsize your library of print-on-paper books.

Important Note: If you are brand new to the Amazon Kindle 2, you may wish to skip ahead and read Parts Two and Three first, as they include some "out of the box" orientation for new Kindle owners.

Part One:

FREE - How to Get Millions of Free Books, Songs, Podcasts, Periodicals & Free eMail, Facebook, Twitter and Wireless Web With Your Amazon Kindle 2

Important Note: If you are brand new to the Amazon Kindle 2, you may wish to skip ahead and read Parts Two and Three first, as they include some "out of the box" orientation for new Kindle owners.

1. Isn't It Ironic? That Expensive Kindle That You're Holding Is the Key to "Free"

Welcome to the Kindlesphere. The Amazon Kindle is that *expensive* ebook reader you've been hearing about: $299 for the Kindle 2, $489 for the super-sized Kindle DX, and $149 for a just-like-new "refurbished" Kindle 1 shipped straight from Amazon.

Who can afford that, especially in these difficult times?

Well, there is a good chance that *you* can. And I'm not just saying that as a balm to heal your potential buyer's remorse if, as is quite possible given the fact that you are reading these lines, you have already bought a Kindle.

The fact is that while the Kindle's entry price may seem a little steep, the Kindle itself is as great a key to future free content of all kinds as you may ever find.

For starters, did you know that the Kindle also comes with a free built-in web browser and a wireless "Whispernet" service that provides you with almost anywhere, anytime connectivity?

Connectivity with Amazon and the Kindle Store, of course, so you can keep buying Kindle books, magazines, newspapers, and blogs, and be reading them on your Kindle within 60 seconds.

Connectivity with Wikipedia, so you can look up anything that comes to mind or that you read about, within seconds.

But that's not all.

You can also connect with Google, with your email or Facebook or Twitter accounts, or with just about any other text-based website!

You can check scores, stocks, news, or weather, and then send an email, a text, or a tweet to share the news.

You can read blogs, online documents, and news sources any time and any place you please.

Don't get me wrong: this is not a lightning-fast, full-featured browser. It's great in a pinch, but you aren't going to start using it to send dozens of email messages each day, watch Youtube videos, or explore Google Earth.

However, it is free, it is there, and it is quiet. If, for instance, you are trying to read a real book on your Kindle, you will find the Kindle's connectivity is a lot less intrusive and distracting than most connected devices. It rests quietly in the background until you decide you need to use it for something.

And at that point, there's no need to find a Starbucks or other wi-fi connection.

There's no need to pay a monthly wireless charge, a data fee, or an activation fee.

There's no need to do anything but enjoy your Kindle.

Free.

But that's just the beginning.

Now that you've purchased this book, you are about to learn about millions of free books, blogs, articles, music tracks, podcasts, periodicals and research documents that you can download to your Kindle in a snap, whether you are stocking up on beach reading or in the middle of a daunting research project.

Whatever you paid for your Kindle, the purpose of this ebook is to provide you with all the information, tips, tricks, and links that you will need to make sure that it begins paying for itself today and continues for each and every day that you use it.

So let's get started.

2. Find and Download Thousands of Free Books From the Kindle Store

Have you heard that most books in the Kindle Store are priced at $9.99?

If so, it might seem like a lot to pay for a digital book, when neither the publisher nor the author incur any expense for printing, paper, shipping, or warehousing. Ebooks at $10 a pop can add plenty to your monthly credit card bill in a hurry.

Well, here's some good news.

Over 40% of the books in the Kindle Store are priced at $4.99 or less, and among those there are – at this writing in September 2009 – over 7,400 free books.

Another 30% are priced between $5 and $10, and of those that are priced above $10, most are technical books whose paper editions are far more expensive.

While it is true that most of the 7,400 free Kindle books are public domain titles, many of these are classics that make great leisure reading. And if you happen to be an English, philosophy, or humanities major, those classics could save you a bundle when it's time to buy textbooks. Not to put too fine a point on this, but these are not junk titles – just type the name of one of your favorite classic authors into your search and you will likely be pleased with the return, especially when you see the prices.

It's easy to access these free book titles and download them to your Kindle within seconds at no charge.

While it's generally true that you will be able to search the Kindle Store more effectively from your computer than from your Kindle, it's certainly possible to get a listing of public domain titles in the Kindle Store while searching with your Kindle. Here are the basics:

From your Kindle, just go to the Kindle Store and type "Public Domain Books" (without the quotation marks) into the search field.

Your Kindle will soon display search results for over 7,000 titles.

If you want to narrow these results by category, just use your Kindle's 5-way to select "Narrow Results by Category" in the upper-right corner of the display screen.

Click on any title to check the price before buying, and select the "Buy" or "Try a Sample" button to download all or part of the book to your Kindle.

As is often the case with Kindle Store searches, you can see a lot more information and make a more informed choice about which books – and which editions – you want to buy or sample if, whenever possible, you do your searching from a computer. Here are a couple of helpful links that will help you find just the kind of free books that you are looking for in the Kindle Store:

- Go to http://bit.ly/FreeKindleStoreBooks for a listing of "over 7,400" free Kindle books of all kinds. Why did I put "over 7,400" in quotation marks? Well, it's because – although there are 7,400 there – Amazon limits your search to 120 pages, so that you may have to surrender after viewing 4,800 free Kindle titles. Do you have to surrender? No, just click on one of the category links in the left sidebar to narrow your search within **specific categories** of free Kindle books.

- Go to http://bit.ly/FreeKindlePromotionalTitles for a listing that excludes all the public domain titles so that you only see those Kindle books whose authors or publishers have set the price at zero, generally as a promotion to stir up interest in a new title or the same author's more recent book.

- While we are at it, you can also get a heads up on Kindle titles that are so new that they have yet to be released just by going to http://bit.ly/ForthcomingKindleTitlesNow, just for fun.

And yes, you can access any of these free titles regardless of which Kindle you may be using, whether you paid $299 for the Kindle 2, $489 for the super-sized Kindle DX, or $199.99 for a just-like-new "refurbished" Kindle 1 shipped straight from Amazon. As a matter of fact, you can even get them without a Kindle if you are equipped with an iPhone or iPod Touch, the free Kindle for iPhone app, and a copy of my 99-cent ebook *No Kindle Required - The Complete "Kindle for iPhone" User's Guide*.

When Amazon began, in August 2009, to limit vendors' ability to offer multiple versions of public domain titles in the Kindle Store, Kindle Nation citizen Diane posted a comment on my blog that I am sure had occurred to many Kindle owners: "I wonder if they are still going to offer all those free/cheap public domain titles."

My take is that Amazon has a strong interest in continuing to provide a healthy catalog of free and cheap titles in the Kindle Store, beginning with its own creation of over 7,300 free offerings last February, for several reasons:

- Free Kindle editions are a strong selling point for Kindle owners, as is evident from the fact that Kindle owners jump all over any link provided here for free books and are, lately, consistently vaulting 15 to 18 free titles at any given time into the top 25 Kindle bestsellers.

- Retail ebook competitors will continue to offer free promotions in an effort to concoct the perfect Kindle-killing recipe.

- Free Kindle editions bring Kindle owners and Kindle for iPhone app users back to the Kindle Store in huge numbers every day, and Amazon knows that most customers will be more likely to buy other things once they have entered the store.

So I think we can safely expect a continued availability of free Kindle books, and many other public domain titles offered at prices between 99 cents and three dollars.

That being said, Kindle owners and the Amazon Kindle Store also have a clear interest in tidying up the Wild West nature of public domain offerings in the Kindle Store, where myriad entrepreneurial ebook publishers have been burdening and cluttering the Kindle catalog with numerous duplicate offerings of material they have lifted from Project Gutenberg (or other sites which have lifted from Project Gutenberg) and published with shoddy formatting and zero editorial value added. Simply by keeping an eye on the count of Kindle book titles, I have seen some recent evidence – at this writing in September 2009 – that Amazon, in addition to scrutinizing newly published titles, is also examining existing texts and dropping some from the catalog.

Then there are the Kindle Store's zero-priced promotional titles, which used to provide a way for indie authors and indie publishers to get some readership attention but in recent months have mainly been restricted to special deals for big publishers or for Amazon's own publications. Hard to say where this will go, or whether Amazon will make the next changes there on its own or under regulatory or legal pressure.

3. Find and Download Free Books From Kindle-Compatible Services (Project Gutenberg's "Magic Catalog," MobileRead, and Feedbooks)

When the Kindle first appeared on the scene late in 2007 many of us – as Kindle owners and authors – moved quickly to find ways to transfer free books from various digital content websites onto our Kindles for reading. Unfortunately, such transfer processes could get a little complicated at times and invariably involved using one's computer and a USB cable as the "middle man" in the process.

Now, in a clear sign that the Kindle has arrived and is well on its way to maturity as an ebook reader, there are several web-based Kindle-compatible services that streamline the process of finding and downloading free books so that you can do this directly from your Kindle almost anywhere, anytime.

The three most prominent and useful of these services, in my experience, are Project Gutenberg's "Magic Catalog," MobileRead, and Feedbooks. The venerable, volunteer-operated, and donation-funded Project Gutenberg is the *sine qua non* of the digital content movement with a vast and growing library of about 30,000 classics and more recently published books, and much of the content on the other services came originally from Project Gutenberg, so it will be my first focus here.

(**Note**: For each of these procedures, I recommend that you start with your Kindle's wireless switched on and that, once you go to the web, you use the Kindle Menu and Settings features to select *Enable Javascript* and *Advanced mode*. To reach the *Basic Web Settings* display screen, press the *Menu* button while you are in the Kindle web browser mode, and select *Settings* with the 5-way or scroll wheel. When you arrive at the *Settings* page, make sure that your Kindle is set to *Advanced Mode* on the top line of this screen (or *Desktop Mode* if you are using the Kindle DX), and to *Enable Javascript*. If you do not anticipate using images as you make use of the Kindle 2 web browser, you can speed up its capacity to process content by selecting *Disable Images* on the bottom line of this display screen.)

The Magic Catalog of Project Gutenberg Ebooks

Project Gutenberg was founded nearly 40 years ago by Michael Hart. Check out its main website at http://www.gutenberg.org and its Wikipedia entry at http://en.wikipedia.org/wiki/Project_Gutenberg to get an appreciation for an inspiring story of a real movement of people committed to a communitarian ideal that has gathered around the work and steadfast commitment of the founding individual. You will also find a PayPal "donate" button on the Project Gutenberg main page and I hope you will do as I try to do and send them a buck now and then even if it means separating the quarters from the lint in your change pocket.

But whether you check out the background information or not, you will find it a snap to turn on your Kindle's wireless feature and download and use The Magic Catalog of Project Gutenberg Ebooks directly with your Kindle. The hardest part of the entire process may be to type the following URL into your Kindle's web browser:

http://freekindlebooks.org/MagicCatalog/MagicCatalog.mobi

However, you probably won't have to do that much typing. First, if you are already reading this content on your Kindle just try moving your Kindle's 5-way to the URL above and clicking. Another alternative, from just about anywhere on your Kindle except the Kindle Store, is to type in a shorter search phrase such as "gutenberg magic catalog" and move the 5-way to the right until you can select Google. With any of these three approaches, you should soon see a link on your Kindle display that reads *Click Here to Download The Magic Catalog of Project Gutenberg Ebooks (MOBI Edition)*.

Once you click on that link your Kindle will prepare to begin to download the Magic Catalog app, and this Dialog box will open on your Kindle display:

Select "ok," of course, and within a moment or two you'll see a document on your Home screen that looks something like this:

The Magic Catalog of Pr...   **Jim Adcock from...**

Just open that "document" and you'll find yourself within a rich catalog of Project Gutenberg files. Initially, until the Kindle system indexes your Magic Catalog, you will be able to search this catalog only by using your Kindle's "PREV PAGE" or "NEXT PAGE" buttons or the Kindle menu's "Go to Location" and "Go to Beginning" features. This can be a slow process. However, once the catalog has been indexed by the Kindle system you'll be able to use your Kindle's powerful search features to type in any keyword, author's name, or title word and view clickable search results within seconds.

Once you find an ebook or other document you wish to read in the Magic Catalog, just select it with your Kindle's 5-way, and you'll see a dialog box like the one in the screen shot shown above. Click "ok" and wait a moment or so. When you see the word "Done" appear at the upper left of the Kindle display, press the "Home" button and, momentarily, you should see the newly downloaded ebook on your Home screen momentarily.

(Note: Just to be clear, nothing in this chapter is meant to imply any affiliation between Project Gutenberg and the Magic Catalog service or any other service. I did check with the good folks at Project Gutenberg on this and received a pleasant and prompt response, to the effect that while there is no affiliation they are glad that the Magic catalog service is opening the door to Project Gutenberg for more Kindle owners).

MobileRead and Feedbooks

These websites provide similar service and selection to the Magic Catalog service for Project Gutenberg. I recommend that you give each of them a look to find the particular service with the presentation, search features, and selection that suits you best.

(Note: Since there is an "automatic download" quality – one that may be a bit faster on the draw than your Kindle's browser or processor – to the sites and services references in this chapter, I recommend that you take an extra step here to avoid confusing your Kindle. If, for instance, the last website you visited before going to the MobileRead site was the Gutenberg Magic Catalog site, try taking a brief detour at another website – any website – before you go to the MobileRead site, so that your Kindle doesn't start downloading from the last site before it brings up the next site. I know, it's a little confusing, but in the long run it may save you a bit of frustration.)

To use **MobileRead**: In your Kindle web browser, type in this URL (or click on the live link if you are reading this on your Kindle):

http://www.mobileread.com/mobiguide

Then click on "Submit" and "Okay" when prompted by your Kindle display. The "Mobiguide Guide" will automatically begin to download to your Kindle, and when the download is complete you'll be able to find "Mobiguide Guide" on your Home Screen. Click on that line to open it, and you'll find a clickable alphabetical listing of authors. You can browse through thousands of public domain titles and seamlessly select the title you want to read. Titles will download to your Kindle and appear on your Home Screen for easy selection and reading.

Feedbooks, at http://www.feedbooks.com/kindleguide, provides a similar service that features thousands of books in Kindle compatible MOBI format. Once you download the "guide" to your Kindle you'll be able to access thousands of public domain titles directly from your Home screen. These MOBI-formatted books look great on the Kindle, and there is even a Kindle help page for Feedbooks visitors at http://www.feedbooks.com/help/kindle. Feedbooks also provides tools for pushing free blog and periodical content to your Kindle and in general is a good service to keep up with.

4. Find Free Books from the Web, Including Any of Google's Million-Plus Free Public Domain Books, and Read Them on Your Kindle

Here's big news for Kindle owners who are trying to balance a hunger to read with, well, the need to balance a budget.

With all the buzz about the millions of public domain books that are available in EPUB format for the new Sony eReaders and other devices via Google Books, one important fact has been missing from the coverage. It's an important fact for Kindle owners, in any case:

It's a snap to download any of these million-plus Google Books public domain books and read them for free right on your Kindle!

That's right. All the noise about EPUB, Google Books, and the Sony Reader somehow amounting to a Kindle Killer somehow manages to miss the basic point that, yeah, *your Kindle can do that!*

Although there are several steps, the entire process only takes a couple of minutes for most books. Here are the steps:

1. Download the amazing ebook conversion program Calibre, set it up and synch it with your Kindle, and keep it on your computer. Calibre is compatible with PCs, Macs, Linux, and the Kindle (among many other devices), and you'll find a detailed description of the service and what it can do for you in Chapters Six and Eight.

2. Go to Google Book Search and select the "Advanced Book Search" link. Although Google does not make it simple to search only for its million-plus free public domain books, you stand a good chance of finding them in any search from this page if you select the buttons for "Full View" and "Books." Although not every "Full

View" book is a public domain book, every free public domain book is a "Full View" book.

3. Fill in any other search criteria that appeal to you, such as author's name, or title, or subject, etc. As with nearly every kind of search, you'll find that you get better with practice at searching Google Books for public domain books to read on your Kindle. You can also broaden your searching process by clicking here to enter the Google Books "Browse" mode, which will return a set of browsing categories such as you might find in the Kindle or Amazon bookstore.

4. When you click on any book's title, you will see a cover or title page display that will allow you to begin reading. If the book is available for download, the download icon will appear just below the upper right corner of the screen. Click on the download icon itself and look for an EPUB link just below it. Click on EPUB, and the download to your computer will begin.

5. Once the book has been downloaded to your computer – a quick process for most books – open the Calibre application on your computer and click on "Add books" from the choices at the top of the Calibre screen. You'll be guided to find and select the book (or books) you have just downloaded.

6. Verify that your Calibre application is set for MOBI output (this setting is displayed just to the right of the big heart on your screen), and then select the "Convert Ebooks" icon near the right of the choices that are arrayed across the top of your Calibre display. Calibre will then display an entry screen that will allow you to make changes in the metadata that will be shown on your Kindle for the book. (Metadata is data that describes a file or document and can be used to search for or sort documents, such as title, author, length, file size, publication date, etc.)

7. Make any changes you wish to make, then click on "OK" at the bottom right, and Calibre will convert your

newly downloaded book to Kindle-compatible MOBI format.

8. Connect your Kindle to your computer, give Calibre a few seconds to recognize your Kindle, and click the "Send to Device" icon near the top of the Calibre display. Once the Calibre hourglass stops rotating in the lower right corner of the display, your new book(s) will be on your Kindle, nicely formatted and ready to read! Just eject the Kindle carefully from your computer, find the new ebook on your Kindle Home screen, and begin reading.

Here are a few notes to keep in mind as you familiarize yourself with this process:

* Although Calibre is very straightforward to use for most purposes, you may well want to go further to get inside the program and see how it works. For that purpose, I recommend some of the user-friendly documentation that Kovid has provided right on the Calibre website, including a thorough and easy-to-follow Calibre User Manual, online; and a FAQ (Frequently Asked Questions) section.

* Once you get the hang of this, you'll also find it easy to streamline the process by converting and downloading multiple books at once.

* Generally, the EPUB to MOBI conversion process works better both with Calibre and with the Kindle than the PDF to MOBI conversion process, or even the Kindle DX PDF reader, but feel free to experiment to see what provides the best results for you.

Read "CellStories" for Free on Your Kindle

Former Akashic Books imprint editor Dan Sinker has created a cool new site called CellStories.net, and it is wonderfully Kindle-friendly in spite of itself. By way of explanation, here's a snippet from the announcement piece that ran on the Publishers Weekly website:

Dan Sinker—founder, editor, Web designer and chief technologist of CellStories.net, a new digital reading venture that offers short narrative content to readers via their cellphones—believes that companies like Amazon and Sony have it all wrong. The future of digital reading, says Sinker, is the cellphone, not dedicated reading devices like the Kindle and the Sony Reader.

So Sinker is launching CellStories: A Daily Dose of Awesome. The venture goes live today and offers short narrative content—1,500-1,700 words of fiction or nonfiction solicited from both published authors and the general public—delivered to consumers through a mobile phone Web site at cellstories.net. Users navigate to the site through the Web browser of their Web-enabled cellphones; the site will offer a different story five days a week, and on the weekend, readers can reread the previous week's offerings.

CellStories runs nicely on the Kindle, and in just a moment I'll provide a quick rundown on how to get CellStories on your Kindle, but first, caveat emptor, or caveat lector, or whatever. Some CellStories offerings are, to say the least, sexually explicit, which is not a deal-breaker for me in any way, but just in case any of my readers think this is a family show, well, I thought I should give fair warning.

Okay then, got that out of the way. If you would like to read CellStories on your Kindle, just follow these steps:

   * Turn on your Kindle and make sure that its Wireless is turned on.

   * Go to the web. A quick way to do this is to type in anything, then click on "google."

   * Once you are on the web, press "Menu" and select "Basic Mode" and "Enter URL." If "Enter URL" is in gray and not clickable, select "Bookmarks," press "Menu" again, and then select "Enter URL".

   * Type in "cellstories.net" and click to the right on "go to". The current CellStories story will open on your Kindle display.

* Read today's story.

* If you like it, press "Menu" and select "Bookmark this page"

And it will be interesting to see how Dan's predictions about the Kindle and cellphones work out. I agree with much that he says, but I suspect that the Kindle hardware and Kindle content will continue to influence what goes on with digital reading, even if – as both of us expect – there ultimately will be millions more people reading on other mobile devices than are reading on Kindles.

Other Free Book Sites

Compared with the fare in the past few chapters, it may seem a bit labor-intensive just to troll the web looking for free books that you can read on your Kindle. But it can also be very rewarding.

While some of the websites that we recommend below will require you to do some reformatting, saving, and transferring to your Kindle via a USB connection with your computer, others are more user-friendly. One that is well worth checking out is the ManyBooks website, where you can explore a remarkable selection of free content that you'll be able to download to your Kindle. This site is wonderfully user-friendly – just find a title by author, title, or the search field, select "Kindle" from the pull-down list of available formats, click on download, and the title will be on your computer drive within seconds. You can shoot it on to your Kindle email address (or transfer it via USB) in another 15 seconds or so.

For a comprehensive list of other websites that feature free content that you can transfer to your Kindle, see the Kindle Nation Daily or A Kindle Home Page blog and scroll down to the "Websites for Free Books" listings in the right sidebar, or use this list directly from your Kindle or other device:

http://bit.ly/FreeKindleStoreBooks
http://bit.ly/FreeKindlePromotionalTitles
http://freekindlebooks.org/MagicCatalog/MagicCatalog.mobi

http://www.mobileread.com/Mobiguide

http://www.feedbooks.com/kindleguide
http://bit.ly/ForthcomingKindleTitlesNow

http://readingroo.ms/

http://www.fictionwise.com/ebooks/freebooks.htm

http://diesel-ebooks.com/cgi-bin/category/free_download

http://www.readprint.com/

Baen Free Library
Creative Commons
Dartmouth College - Ebooks in the Public Domain
Digital Book Index
Free Techbooks
Google Book Search
Internet Archive
Librivox
MobileRead
Munseys
Online Books Page
Podiobooks
Project Gutenberg
Technical Books Online
Wikibooks
World Public Library
Wowio

For most of these free book websites, the process is quite simple: just download a book to your computer using the instructions found on the site, and transfer the book to your Kindle. You can send any such file directly and wirelessly to your Kindle via your you@kindle.com email address. Keep in mind that Amazon will charge you at least 15 cents a pop for the conversion to the Kindle's AZW format and the Whispernet blast, more if the file is larger than one megabyte. I greatly prefer using the elegant but free Calibre service, which is described in Chapter 6.

5. Find and Download Free Book Samples and Free 14-Day Periodical Trials From the Kindle Store

While it is certainly true that a Kindle in the hands of an avid reader like you or me can quickly lead to some significant expenditures for reading materials, it is also true that Amazon has designed the Kindle and arranged the Kindle Store to make it easy for us to sample any Kindle edition before we buy it. Once you get the hang of using the free sample chapters for Kindle books or the 14-day free trials for blogs and periodicals, you may find that they provide you with a great way to look before you buy.

First, try out the Kindle's terrific **sampling** feature. Whether you're browsing titles directly from your Kindle or on your computer, the Kindle edition detail page for just about any title in the Kindle Store will show a button on the right that allows you to send a sample chapter or two (usually between 5 and 10 per cent of the full text) directly, and pretty much instantly, to your Kindle. What's not to like about that?

The sample will download directly and wirelessly to your Kindle just like the complete book would, and the title will be displayed on your Home screen with the word "Sample" in a small font just to the left of the title line.

Once you have a sample on your Kindle, it's easy to make a buying decision directly from your Kindle either by pressing the menu button and selecting "Buy this Book Now" or by going to the end of the sample where you'll find a link to buy the book.

One important warning: don't necessarily assume that a book that you have sampled will continue to be offered at the same price that you noted when you first looked at it in the Kindle Store. For this and other reasons, I usually look at a book's Kindle Store product page on my computer before clicking to buy rather than clicking to buy it from my Kindle or while reading the sample.

Perhaps because of confusion between the Kindle books free sample program and the free 14-day trials for periodicals and blogs, some Kindle owners have been confused about whether book samples might automatically roll over and morph into purchases. For instance, Elizabeth from Fort Worth wrote in, on Amazon's discussion page for one of my books: "If you leave your sample on [your Kindle] too long, will they eventually charge you for it?"

Elizabeth, Amazon should never charge you for a sample of a Kindle book. If you feel you have been charged wrongly, it's worth a call to the Kindle Customer Support number at 1-866-321-8851 to seek redress. Be sure to have the identifying information for the charge in front of you when you call.

However, if you sign up for the "sample" form of a Kindle blog, newspaper, or magazine, which is a 14-day free trial, charges will begin immediately after 14 days unless you cancel the free trial before the end of that period.

Also keep in mind:

- You can't easily cancel a Kindle periodical with your Kindle. Instead, go to your Manage Your Kindle page on Amazon.com from your computer. Scroll down to "Your active Kindle subscriptions" and you'll find it easy to cancel any subscription using the link to its right. (If you have a lot of Kindle subscriptions and you want to see them all at once without going through intermediate steps and extra clicks, use this link to see Manage Your Kindle Subscriptions in "View All" mode.

- If a 14-day free trial ends and Amazon begins charging you for the subscription, all is not lost. You can still cancel the subscription following the same process outlined in the paragraph above, and Amazon will refund – at the least – the pro-rated amount for the portion of the subscription month that you haven't received yet.

- In my personal experience, I've actually noticed that a few of my mid-month cancellations of Kindle periodical or blog subscriptions have resulted in a full rather than a partial refund. For those of us who keep track of small change, that's found money.

6. Use Calibre to Manage Your Kindle's Free Books and Other Kindle Content

Any Kindle owners interested in getting the most out of free content on the Kindle should make a point of getting familiar with the greatest Kindle app to come along yet, called Calibre.

Calibre provides features for a wide range of different ebook platforms and devices, but the fact that it supports the Kindle so elegantly is bound to make it a favorite with Kindle owners. In this chapter we will focus on Calibre's usefulness in managing, accessing, reading, and maintaining accurate metadata for the ebooks that you may have acquired based on the tips in Chapters 2, 3, and 4.

According to its creator Kovid Goyal, Calibre was designed to make organizing your ebook collection as easy as possible. It can also be used to manage books, magazines, newspapers, comics and virtually any other kind of digital content. And, like most of the files that you will be handling with Calibre, the Calibre application itself is free.

The Calibre application will reside on your computer and will provide a great interface between your computer and your Kindle that will make it easy for you to do any of the following:

- Convert ebooks and documents from other formats – including CBZ, CBR, CBC, EPUB, FB2, HTML, LIT, MOBI, ODT, PDF, PRC, PDB, PML, RB, RTF, and TXT – either to MOBI format so that you can read them on your Kindle or to a wide variety of other formats so that you can read them on your computer or on another mobile device. These other formats include EPUB, FB2, OEB, LIT, LRF, MOBI, PDB, PML, RB, PDF, and TXT.

- Read any supported ebook format directly from the Calibre ebook viewer on your computer.

- Send ebooks to directly to your Kindle library via USB cable without any need to pay for Amazon's conversion process.

- Make corrections or changes in the "metadata" – such as titles, authors' and publishers' names, publication date, tags, ratings, and other data – that are associated with each of the ebooks on your Kindle. Without getting too far afield from the basic subject at hand here – free content – you may find that this ability to edit metadata can be a powerful tool in sorting, organizing, and managing the content on your Kindle.

In order to begin using Calibre, you'll need to download the app to your computer. You can download the Calibre software in formats that are compatible, respectively, with Windows, OS X for the Mac, or Linux at http://calibre.kovidgoyal.net/download.

I recommend that, even before you download Calibre, you begin by watching Kovid's YouTube presentation on Calibre at http://bit.ly/CalibreVideo. As much as it is my usual style to go through and break down instructional material step-by-step, the fact that Calibre is still in beta – Version 0.6.10 as I write this – suggests to me that it will be more beneficial to you, now that I hope that I have whetted your appetite about what Calibre can do for you and walked you to the front door of the Calibre site, if I simply suggest that you watch Kovid's video and review the material on the site. In the future, you may also want to check out YouTube's eReader channel at http://bit.ly/eReaders-on-YouTube to look for more recent presentations.

Once you download and open Calibre, you'll find a very hospitable Welcome Wizard that will prompt you to designate a directory where you will store and manage your Calibre Library off-Kindle so that you can begin taking advantage of the app's powerful feature set. Naturally, you'll find that you have the greatest range of ebook management options for those files that are not restricted by Digital Rights Management, a subject that we'll explore in Chapter 14.

Although Calibre is very straightforward to use for most purposes, you may well want to go further to get inside the program and see how it works. For that purpose, I recommend some of the user-friendly documentation that Kovid has provided right on the Calibre website, including a thorough and easy-to-follow Calibre User Manual, online; and a FAQ (Frequently Asked Questions) section.

7. Read Blogs, Periodicals, and Other Web Content for Free on the Kindle

Amazon might prefer that you get all your Kindle blogs and periodicals for a price in the Kindle Store, and those Kindle editions are tough to match when it comes to elegant formatting and the convenience of having new issues and posts pushed wirelessly to your Kindle in real time. However, there are a number of increasingly user-friendly ways to enjoy newspapers, magazines, and blogs free of charge on a Kindle, and we'll break them down and show you how in this chapter and the next.

Here are the basic approaches:

- You can use your Kindle's web browser to read any of millions of blogs and online editions directly from the web.

- You can use any of several RSS feed services such as Google Reader to read content summaries on your Kindle and then click through to content that interests you.

- You can use Instapaper to flag interesting articles as you surf the web and send them individually or in digest form to your Kindle.

- You can set up Calibre to fetch the latest issues of newspapers, magazines and blogs and transfer them directly to your Kindle via an easy-to-use Calibre-to-Kindle USB connection.

We'll focus on the first three options in this chapter, and then focus solely on Calibre – my favorite application for these purposes – in the next chapter.

Reading Directly on the Web
With the Kindle Web Browser

Kindle owner preferences vary widely as to whether they enjoy reading online content directly with the Kindle's web browser. I find that it can be very convenient, in a pinch, to use my Kindle to check or read some material that is important to me on the web, especially if I am away from my computer or an internet connection. The price is always right and the connection is quiet and inconspicuous so that nobody else is likely to notice if I divert my attention now and then during a less than scintillating meeting to check my Kindle for the score of a game that is in progress, the latest news, any new emails I may have received, or a stock price.

The extent to which such browsing, checking, and reading suits one's purposes usually depends on several things:

- A website's balance between text and graphics, since graphic-intensive websites are generally very slow to load on a Kindle and difficult to view on the Kindle 1 or the Kindle 2.

- How much content is involved. Unless one is viewing the web in landscape view and desktop mode on a Kindle DX, many web pages do not automatically format very well on a Kindle screen. I don't mind putting up with some sloppy formatting if I am reading a paragraph or two, but when I am reading a 2,000-word New York Times article I prefer the kind of user-friendly formatting that I am accustomed to either with the Kindle edition of the Times or with the Calibre fetch process.

- Whether real-time updates are involved. For instance, using the mobile MLB.com site to check on my beloved Red Sox either during or after a game works very well on the Kindle.

- Whether the particular websites that you frequent provide a stripped-down, user-friendly presentation for mobile devices.

- One's general patience and tolerance for the relatively slow web page downloads and occasional freezes that one experiences with the Kindle.

But I heartily recommend that you give the Kindle's web browser a try so that you can see if there are specific websites for which it works well in your daily life or, say, if you are vacationing for a week in a rustic, wifi-free cottage among the Outer Cape's dunes. In order to help you find websites that work well for you and your Kindle and appeal to your specific interests, I'll provide an index here to the list of hundreds of Kindle-ready web links that appears later in this book:

Kindle Store, app, and Kindle Essential Links

Freebies for Your Kindle

Amazon Store Bestseller Links

Best Blogs

Blog Lists

Book Catalogs

Book Reviews

Business & Finance

Comics

eBook Downloads, Support & Discussions

Entertainment

Hobbies

Kindle Blogs

Kindle Gear

Magazines

Mail & Message

Mobile RSS Readers

Mobile Transcoders

Mobile Site Lists

Newspapers

News: National

News: Sports

News: Technology

Reference

Shipping Carriers
Shopping
Travel
Weather

To help simplify the process, I recommend that you reorganize your Kindle's web browser bookmarks as follows:

- Open the web browser. (I find that the easiest way to do this is to type anything – like "web" – into the Kindle and move the 5-way to the right to select "google." The Kindle begins a Google search for whatever is typed in, but more importantly, the browser is open.)

- Once you are in the browser, press the Menu button and select "Bookmarks."

- When your list of web bookmarks appears on the Kindle display, delete some of the bookmarks that you'll probably never use. For me, for instance, that meant deleting the bookmarks for Google and Wikipedia because it is far easier to open Google and Wikipedia from within the Kindle's onboard search (as described in the example two paragraphs above), and deleting some other bookmarks such as those for E! Online and a recipe website because, well, I just know that I'll never use them.

- Deleting a bookmark with the Kindle 2 or Kindle DX is an easy process. Just move the 5-way to the bookmark's line in the bookmark list, but instead of pressing down to select and open the bookmark, move the 5-way to the left to begin the deletion process and follow the onscreen dialog box.

- By deleting bookmarks that you won't use, you create space on the first page of your Kindle web bookmarks display to add, judiciously, the bookmarks that you're most likely to frequent. Take some care with this process, because (to the best of my knowledge) you won't be able to change the order of appearance for whatever bookmarks populate your list: the list will always display with the bookmarks that you've kept from the original list in their originbal order, followed by the bookmarks that you add in the order that you add them.

- In order to add a bookmark you must first go to the web page you want to bookmark, either by typing in the URL, finding it through a Google or other search, or using your 5-way to click on a link in something you are reading on your Kindle.

- Once you are viewing a web page on your Kindle, you can easily add a bookmark for the page just by pressing the Menu button and selecting "Bookmark this page." (Note: If you seek to bookmark more than one page from a particular domain – as I have occasionally done with Google Mobile features – you may occasionally run into a conflict when multiple bookmarks are read by your Kindle as having the same metadata title. I know of no solution for this problem other than to select my one best choice from these pages as the one which I'll bookmark).

Setting Up a Google Reader RSS Feed for Your Kindle

What is Google Reader? Google Reader is yet another nifty web-based service from Google. It aggregates content through RSS feeds from the web, based on each individual's tastes and selections, and serves the content in real time to an individual's personal Google Reader page for reading online or offline. It is compatible through web browser platforms with a wide variety of devices, including the Kindle. For a simple and useful 3-minute video about Google Reader in plain English, see the CommonCraft video at http://www.commoncraft.com/rss_plain_english.

Using Google Reader To Read Your Favorite Blogs on the Kindle. For many Kindle owners, the Kindle is all about convenience, and there is nothing at all wrong with that. When it comes to reading blogs on the Kindle, you may be perfectly content to pay a small monthly fee for the experience. You may even be satisfied with Amazon's selection of (at this writing) 6,947 blogs. If you're satisfied, you need not read further.

50

But if you're the kind of independent-minded reader who prefers to **make your own selections** and you prefer not to be charged money for content that is intended by its authors to be available **free of charge**, there is another way.

By following the few, very easy steps outlined in this chapter, you can adapt Google Reader to your Kindle so that it fetches the blog content that you're most interested in reading and pushes that content right to your Kindle's web browser where you may read it anywhere, anytime, and at absolutely no cost.

Set Up Your Google Accounts. The first step, if you haven't already done so, is to establish a Google account. As you follow various suggestions in this book for making the most of your Kindle, it's very likely that you'll be using several features of your Google account, including Google Reader, Gmail, Google Blog Search, Google Search, Google Notebook, Google Calendar, Blogger, and Google News. Although we're still early in the Age of the Kindle, it's becoming increasingly clear that, whether or not Google and Amazon ever enter into any explicit joint agreement regarding services that optimize the Kindle, Google will be a steady source for useful enhancements for Kindle owners.

All of Google's services can be accessed through a single Google user account. For most people, the most convenient approach will be to use the same Google account with your Kindle that you use on your desktop or notebook computer. However, there may be some circumstances in which it is useful to employ separate accounts for different devices. For instance, if you use Google Reader to follow multimedia-intensive blogs on your computer, you may want to use a separate account for subscriptions to the more text-intensive blogs that are suitable for Kindle reading.

Bookmark Your Google Mobile And Google Reader Pages. Creating bookmarks for Google Reader and other mobile Google services in your Kindle's web browser will save you and your thumbs a lot of extra work in the future, and it is an easy process.

1. Make sure that your Kindle's Whispernet wireless feature is turned on.

2.   From your Kindle's "Home" screen, press the "Menu" button on the right edge of the Kindle.

3.   Use the 5-way to select "Experimental" from the menu selections, and then choose "Basic Web" from the "Experimental" page.

4.   Once you are in the web browser, press the "Menu" button again and use the 5-way to click on "Settings" from the menu selection. On the web browser's Settings page, enable (or verify that you have already enabled) Javascript and "Advanced" Mode (rather than "Default" Mode). (Note: The web browser's Settings page is different from the Settings page accessible directly from your Kindle's "Home" screen.)

5.   Click on "Enter URL" at the top of the next screen and type the following into the input field to the right of the "http://" prefix:

m.google.com

6.   When the Google Mobile products page loads onto your Kindle screen, move the 5-way up or down to enter cursor mode and push down twice quickly on the 5-way to bookmark the Google Mobile products page.

7.   From the Google Mobile products page, use the 5-way to select "Reader" from the Google Mobile products choices.

8.   When the Google Reader page loads onto your Kindle screen, move the 5-way up or down to enter cursor mode and push down twice quickly on the 5-way to bookmark the Google Reader page.

You will then have bookmarks for the top-level Google Mobile products page and for the Google Reader page. You may, of course, follow similar steps to bookmark other Google pages that you expect to use.

How to Subscribe to Your Favorite Blogs With Google Reader. Generally speaking, you'll find it much easier to use your computer, rather than your Kindle, to search out your favorite blogs and add them to your Google Reader subscriptions so that you can then have easier access to them on your Kindle. It's an easy process:

1. Find a blog that you want to add to your Google Reader subscriptions. Find the RSS Feed button on the blog and copy it. (In many cases, you can simply type the blog's URL into the input field rather than looking for an RSS Feed button).

2. Open the main Google Reader page. The shortest URL that I have found for this is reader.google.com. If you haven't already signed in with your Google account, do so.

3. From the "sidebar" column to the left of your Google Reader screen, select the **Add Subscriptions** link.

4. Copy the RSS feed link of the blog to which you want to subscribe into the input field that opens when you select the **Add Subscriptions** link. The blog will now be included in your Google Reader subscriptions. (As noted above, in many cases, you can simply type the blog's URL into the input field rather than looking for an RSS Feed button).

How to Read Blogs on the Kindle With Google Reader. Once you've completed to the steps above, reading blogs on the Kindle is remarkably simple and user-friendly.

1. Make sure that your Kindle's Whispernet wireless feature is turned on.

2. From your Kindle's "Home" screen, press the "Menu" button on the right edge of the Kindle.

3. Use the 5-way to select "Experimental" from the menu selections, and then choose "Basic Web" from the "Experimental" page.

4. Choose "Google Reader" from your Kindle web browser's bookmarks (the bookmark is there

because you followed the steps in an earlier section to create it). The Bookmarks page is the "default" page that usually appears first when you enter the web browser, but if another page comes up instead, just push the "Menu" button (within the web browser) and use the 5-way to select "Bookmarks."

5. When the "Google Reader" page loads to your Kindle screen, you may be required to provide the log-in name and password of your Google account, but generally you'll only be required to do this when your browser's cache has been cleared either manually or by a system reset. Once you log in, you are ready to start reading.

6. In order to "sort" your blogs and read only the posts on a particular blog, just click on "Subscriptions" from the "Google Reader" page and select the blog you wish to read. Generally, this will create a more pleasurable reading experience than jumping from one subject matter to another. (It may also protect you from losing track of the content on a two-posts-per-day blog that might otherwise be overwhelmed by more frequent posts from other, more prolific blogs.)

Flag & Send Interesting Web Content with Instapaper

Here's another cool web-based service that is primarily designed for Kindle owners. It makes it stunningly easy and convenient to grab interesting content on the fly from any website and read it later on your Kindle.

Just go to Instapaper.com, sign up for a free account, and link your account to your Kindle via your You@kindle.com email address. Grab the "Read Here" button, stick it on your browser's toolbar and you are ready to go. Wherever you surf on the web all day long, you can click that "Read Here" link and the content that you select will be sent to your Kindle, all in a reader-friendly digest file that will be easy to identify on your Home screen, whenever you want: on demand, once a day, or once a week.

Please note: Amazon will charge you 15 cents per Instapaper transmission and conversion to your Kindle via your You@kindle.com email address, as well as an additional 15 cents for each megabyte of the file's size beyond the first megabyte of any file.

8. Fetch the News, Newspapers and Magazines, And Other Content with Calibre

In Chapter 6 you learned how to use Calibre to manage your ebook library. In this chapter, we'll focus on how you can send Calibre out onto the web to fetch entire periodicals on a regular basis online and, then, to deliver them in elegantly formatted files directly to your Kindle.

Once you have Calibre open on your computer, it's a snap to fetch free content from a growing list of great online sources. To get started, just click on the "Fetch news" icon near the top of the Calibre display and select "Schedule news download" from its pulldown menu:

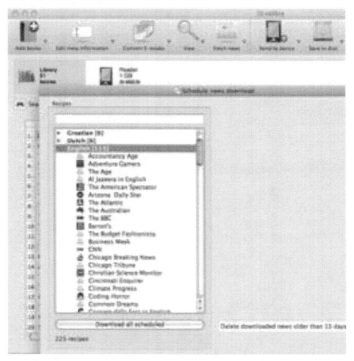

The next display to appear on your screen allows you to select the language in which you wish to find online content. If you click on "English," you'll see a list of content choices such as the one above. Just click on the periodical of your choice and Calibre will display dialog boxes to prompt you through the process of setting your preferences for scheduling regular downloads of its content at a time of your choice daily or on a certain day or days each week. The choice of the download time can be important for several reasons:

* You may want to make sure that a daily newspaper downloads at the optimal time to catch its most recent edition, such as 5 a.m.

* You'll need to have Calibre open on your computer in order to complete your "Fetch news" downloads on schedule.

* You'll need to ensure that your Kindle is connected to your computer via USB cable if you want Calibre to push your scheduled "Fetch news" downloads automatically to your Kindle on schedule.

Try it. I think you'll like it, and you may be amazed at how nicely and fully Calibre renders your "Fetch News" content on your Kindle. For instance, the weekly fetch of *The New Yorker* comes complete with the new issue's cartoons, Goings on About Town listings, and helpful article summaries.

Please note: Although Calibre is very straightforward to use for most purposes, you may well want to go further to get inside the program and see how it works. For that purpose, I recommend some of the user-friendly documentation that you'll find right on the Calibre website, including a thorough and easy-to-follow online Calibre User Manual and a FAQ (Frequently Asked Questions) section.

9. Use Kindle Nation Daily's Free Book Alerts

Okay, you can call this a commercial if you want, because I'm touting my own Kindle Nation Daily blog, but at least it's a commercial that will lead you to even more free books and content for your Kindle.

Several times a week you'll find new listings of free content at Kindle Nation Daily. So, if you are interested in keeping up with what's free and what's worth reading in the Kindlesphere, as well as hundreds of other useful tips and tricks for getting the most out of your Kindle, you should definitely sign up for my free weekly email newsletter, Kindle Nation, at the Kindle Nation Archive site at http://bit.ly/KindleNationArchive.

Or, if you want a little more Kindle-compatible convenience for just 99 cents a month, you can have each and every Kindle Nation Daily post pushed directly to your own Kindle in real time by subscribing to http://bit.ly/KindleNationDaily in the Kindle Store. Kindle Nation regularly provides information on late-breaking freebies in the Kindle Store, and for 99 cents a month your Kindle edition subscription will ensure that you receive this information before it's too late to act on it.

10. Unlock the World
Of Free Audio on the Kindle

On the Kindle, "Free" doesn't apply only to *visual text*.

Your Kindle also makes it easy to listen to several different kinds of content in audio form, and much of this is, like so much else we have described in this book, is free. You'll find it easy to transfer MP3 versions of your favorite music, podcasts, and radio shows and listen to them free on your Kindle, and of course you'll also find that many of the free books and other files that you download from the Kindle Store or from other sources suggested in this book work nicely with the text-to-speech feature on the Kindle 2 or Kindle DX.

But there's more, and what better place to start than with a website called BooksShouldBeFree.com?

Free Audio Books, No Robot Included

I'll admit it: I love listening to the newspaper in Kindle Robot-speak (the "woman" is so much better than the "man", but that might just be my quirky personal taste for, well, clear enunciation), but there aren't many books that I would like to have read to me in such an obviously disembodied voice.

Audible.com is wonderfully convenient to use, but some may find it a bit expensive. So I was happy to stumble upon a website called BooksShouldBeFree.com, where real human beings do a great job of reading great books. Check it out and you'll probably find it as easy as I did to download a book or two to your computer. Once you've done that, you'll see that the files usually are broken up by chapter, so you can transfer a chapter or two at a time to your Kindle without using up too much storage space. Over the weekend I sampled both the first chapter and Molly's soliloquy from Ulysses, and found the readings delightful.

Now that Amazon has launched its remarkable "Read-to-Me" feature for the Kindle 2 and Kindle DX, it would be easy to overlook the device's other audio features, but they are still significant and they can add to your enjoyment of any member of the Kindle family.

Using Your Kindle as an Audio Device

Okay, it's all well and good to whet your appetite with the promise that you can listen not only to text-to-speech but also to countless other free audio books, music tracks, podcasts, and radio programs with your Kindle. But I haven't given you much guidance yet about how to do it, right? So let's take care of that, with:

* A basic description of Kindle audio.

* A guide to the Kindle's "Play MP3" feature that lets you play background music as you read.

* A description of how you can use the Kindle's "Audible" folder and features to exercise greater control while listening to any MP3 audio file (not just those you download from Audible.com!)

The basics of Kindle audio. Every Kindle comes with a built-in MP3 player and works seamlessly as a listening device for various kinds of listening files. The stereo speakers mounted at the bottom rear of the Kindle 2 may not impress you, but they are a big improvement over the tinny, barely audible external sound that emitted from the Kindle 1, and the Kindle DX audio is even stronger and richer. To go one step better, you can use the audio-jack to the right of the power switch on the top edge of the Kindle to connect it to a speaker or headset. On the right edge, you will find "down" and "up" volume-control buttons. (I would go so far as to say that headphones or some other sort of external speaker are a must if you are using a first-generation Kindle, also known as a Kindle 1).

How to use the Kindle's "Play MP3" feature to play background music as you read. For uses other than the "Read-to-Me" feature and listening to Audible.com files, the Kindle nomenclature for its audio functionality is "Play MP3," and it will work only with podcasts, music, or other audio files that are in an MP3 format and are not DRM-protected. (Although Kindle users often think of DRM or Digital Rights Management as an ebook issue, much of the world learned of DRM first in connection with music. For a good explanation of what is involved with DRM and music, see http://bit.ly/MusicDRM-Explainer.)

In order to get listening material onto your Kindle you must transfer it from your computer, using the Kindle's USB cable, into your Kindle's native "music" file. Just find the file (or files) on your computer using the computer's "Finder" or "My Computer" application, copy it, and paste it into your Kindle's "music" folder. Such files will often be found in your "My Music" folder, in a downloads folder, or on your computer's desktop. Pay attention to your Kindle's storage capacity and remaining storage space, as audio files require much more storage space than text files. You can always check the remaining space available on your Kindle by pressing the "Menu" button and reading the "xxxx MB free" line to the left of the time on the top line of the display.

Once you have listening files in the "music" folder on board your Kindle, you can begin or end use of the Kindle's audio feature by holding down the "ALT" key on your Kindle keyboard and pressing the spacebar.

While listening to your Kindle's music or podcast files in Play MP3 mode, you'll generally be operating blind, since the Kindle plays whatever is in its listening queue either in shuffle or sequential order (based on the order you transferred the files to your Kindle) without any onscreen reference. However, you can press the ALT+F key at any time to skip to the next track, and pause or resume play by pressing ALT+Spacebar. The Kindle's MP3 player will continue to play if it's playing when you put your Kindle to sleep, but you won't be able to use these keyboard commands with the MP3 player unless you awaken your Kindle again.

I find the best way to manage the music I want to hear on my Kindle is to create several "playlist" folders in the top-level Kindle directory, each representing an appropriate selection for a particular situation. I might listen to jazz while reading a book, or something a bit more lyric-intensive while reading *The New York Times*. By moving a certain playlist into the Kindle's "music" folder – the only folder from which the Kindle will recognize and play music – I can suit my listening to my situation in a couple of key strokes while the Kindle is connected to my computer. However, it's worth mentioning again that sound files can take up a large percentage of the Kindle's memory, so it may make sense to keep some of these files off-Kindle in a Kindle-management folder accessible through your computer's "Finder" or "My Computer" functions.

It's also a simple matter, retracing these same steps, to listen to podcasts on my Kindle once I move them from my computer to the Kindle's "music" folder.

How to use the Kindle's "Audible" folder and features to exercise greater control while listening to audio books, podcasts, music or any MP3 audio file (not just those you download from Audible.com). Although it's a pretty well-kept secret, you can also use the Kindle's "audible" folder to play any audio file as long as you aren't going to be reading or making use of other features on your Kindle while you're listening. Two great things about this particular mode of listening are:

> * The file will be listed on your Home screen (with the word "audio" to the left of the title).

> * You can use the same full set of features to navigate or replay the audio files that are available to you while listening to an Audible.com file, or for that matter, an iTunes file.

This "audible" listening mode can be especially useful for a handful of favorite songs or for listening to a podcast such as Len Edgerly's weekly The Kindle Chronicles on your Kindle. The ability to use the Kindle 5-way to go back or forward 30 seconds in a podcast makes this mode a pleasure to use.

Whether you follow your favorite podcasts directly from the web (as with the link to The Kindle Chronicles) or download them through iTunes, it's easy to transfer them to your Kindle's

"Audible" folder. For instance, because I have subscribed to NPR favorite Ira Glass' This American Life podcast on iTunes, iTunes automatically downloads an MP3 file of each week's show to a folder (Music>iTunes>iTunesMusic>Downloads>Podcasts>This American Life) on my iMac. Then I just go to that folder, copy the most recent file, paste it in my Kindle's "audible" folder, and I'm good to go.

I can do the same with any other DRM-free MP3 audio file that resides on my computer's hard drive, including, for instance, tracks that I have downloaded to my iTunes folders from CDs that I have purchased and music files – like the Mozart tracks mentioned in the next section – that I have purchased from Amazon's MP3 Downloads Store.

All you have to do to opt for this "audible" mode is copy and paste an audio file into your Kindle's "audible" folder rather than its "music" folder. Then, once you eject the Kindle from your computer connection, you will find the "audible" folder's new file(s) toward the end of your Home screen display of titles, with the word "audio" to the left of each title line. Just click on the title and you'll see easy-to-use listening controls right on your Kindle display.

Later in this chapter we'll also take a look at Audible.com itself since, if you're an audible.com subscriber, you'll frequently receive offers of **free Audible.com audiobooks** that can be downloaded to your Kindle.

Mozart on Your Kindle: Getting the Most out of Kindle Audio

Let's say that, like many Kindle owners, you are a bit more of a reader than a rocker. Or not. But if you are yet to make much use of the Kindle's audio features, let's walk through a simple and inexpensive process that could provide you with hours of delightful Mozart classics as background music while you read your favorite books or periodicals on your Kindle, all for a grand total of $7.99 and very little expenditure of time. What's not to like about that?

The Kindle MP3 player plays music and podcasts in non-DRM .mp3 format. While it might be nice if you can purchase such content and have it sent wirelessly to your Kindle, audio file sizes and transfer speeds make this unlikely. However, it's easier and cheaper than you may think to purchase reading-friendly background music, transfer it to your Kindle, and start listening.

If you like Wolfgang Amadeus Mozart, start by going to the Amazon page for The 99 Most Essential Mozart Masterpieces, a collection that features hours of wonderful Mozart compositions performed by the world's greatest orchestras and soloists. While it's possible to purchase the individual tracks for 89 cents each, you can spend a total of $7.99 and get all 99 tracks, ranging in length from under two minutes to longer than 15 minutes, just by clicking on the orange "Buy MP3 album with 1-click" button near the upper-right corner of your computer screen. Amazon will begin downloading the album almost immediately, perhaps after asking you to enable the Amazon downloader tool to work on your computer if you haven't done so already. Keep track of where your computer saves the album download. This will usually be in a folder or directory called "Music" that is associated with your default audio program such as iTunes or Windows Media Player.

Once the album downloads to your computer, plug your Kindle into your computer via the USB cable. From within your computer's "Finder" or "My Computer" feature, locate the music files that were just downloaded, select the tracks that you want to copy to your Kindle, and pick them up with the **Copy** command. (**Important Note**: Remember that audio files require more storage capacity than text, and *don't overdo it*. I recommend that you choose a dozen or two of the tracks you think you'll enjoy the most and copy them rather than trying to store all 99 tracks on your Kindle!)

Next, go to the Kindle folder from your computer's "Finder" or "My Computer" structure, open it, and then open the subfolder called "music." Use your system's **Paste** command to paste the music tracks into your Kindle's "music" folder, eject the Kindle from your computer, and you are ready to enjoy some nice background music as you read. Just press Home to go to the Kindle 2 Home screen, press Menu, then use the 5-way to select

"Experimental" and "Play MP3" from the next two menus that appear on your Kindle display.

Listening to Free Audible.com Content on Your Kindle

If you have tired a bit of listening to the gradually improving but still seemingly robotic voice of text-to-speech on the Kindle 2 or Kindle DX, perhaps it's time to treat yourself to the pleasure of listening to a favorite book read by the author or a professional actor via Audible.com.

In a previous section I provided instructions for listening to any podcast, song, or other audio file with the full suite of audiobook controls associated with your Kindle's audible folder, as opposed to using your Kindle's "background music" Play MP3 feature set.

But actual audiobooks from Audible.com are a treat.

You can listen either on your Kindle or on a computer or other device, and you can get one audiobook for free with Audible.com's 14-day free trial.

When you enter Audible.com for the first time as a Kindle user at http://www.audible.com/kindle you will be invited to get a **free Audible.com book** as a Gold plan customer with **a free month of Audible.com service.** Once you have signed up you'll be prompted to download your first book for free from among 60,000 choices.

Be sure to make a note of the date on which your 14-day trial period ends so that you can log in and opt out of your Audible.com membership before any charges are applied to your account.

Or, if you're like me, you may find enough to like about being an Audible.com member to hold onto it at $14.99 a month (or less if you pay for a year in advance).

Part of what keeps me loving Audible.com are the treats that I find when I click "Free for Members" from the menu bar near the top of my main Audible.com page. That link directs me to all kinds of goodies being promoted by Audible.com, including a free subscription to the daily digital audio version of *The New York Times*.

Once you spring for Audible.com membership – which begins at $12.46 per month, for an annualized Audible Listener Gold account – you may be amazed at the hundreds of free audiobooks that are available to you. To browse the possibilities, just go to Audible.com, click on the Advanced Search link in the upper left corner, and select "**Free**" from the pull-down menu in the Price field.

Unlike Kindle edition books that can be purchased and downloaded directly from, and with, your Kindle, you'll need to use your computer to purchase and download content from Audible.com. (Since Amazon purchased Audible.com around the time of the Kindle launch, it's fair to expect that Audible.com connectivity for Kindle users may well be enhanced at some point in the future, but the difficulty that must be overcome both for Audible.com and Amazon MP3 content involves file size and the resulting effect on transfer speed).

For now, purchase your content and use the free Audible Manager software on the site to download it to your computer, then transfer the content to your Kindle's native "audible" folder using your USB connection. If you are using a Mac, you may not be able to download Audible.com content unless you are using Windows-emulation software. When prompted by Audible Manager to select your listening device's "Audio Format Sound Quality," you can choose 2, 3 or 4 for Kindle compatibility. The best quality, and the largest file size, comes with selection 4 – whether you choose this option may depend on your download speed and on the file space you have available on your Kindle.

Navigate to http://www.audible.com/kindle and sign up if you have not done so already. Download the Audible Manager software to your computer and re-start your web browser. Connect your Kindle to your computer via USB and "activate" the Kindle as your listening device within Audible Manager. After you purchase listening content, you'll be able to copy it to your Kindle and listen to it there.

Once you've transferred Audible content to your Kindle, you should be able to access it directly from your Home screen with your 5-way, just as you would a Kindle book or other content. Look for a tiny speaker icon next to the Audible.com content.

After you've opened an Audible.com file, just use the onscreen navigation menu to move among your options including Beginning, Previous Section, Next Section, Back 30 Seconds, Forward 30 Seconds, and a Play/Pause toggle.

You'll have several listening options, including the Kindle's onboard stereo speakers. For better sound quality, use the audio jack to the left of the USB slot at the bottom of the Kindle to connect it to a speaker or headset. That jack will also work if you have an automobile with an MP3 jack. Further to the right of the Kindle's bottom edge, you will find "down" and "up" volume-control buttons. (Tip: If you don't do a lot of Kindle listening and your first Audible file doesn't seem to be starting for you, make sure that the volume is turned up.)

And everything that you find there transfers easily to your Kindle's "audible" folder with the instructions found earlier in this chapter.

11. Use Free Email, Facebook, Twitter And Other Services on the Kindle

When I was a kid my mother used to buy produce off the back of a truck that came through our Jamaica Plain neighborhood each afternoon. It was fresh and inexpensive, and you found out what was available each day when you heard the leather lungs of the vendor calling out "Fresh tomatoes! Snap peas! Green beans! Bananas! Cantaloupes!"

Everybody on Brookley Road needed something from that list, and the guy did a good business.

Imagine if he came back to the hip, young professional neighborhood that characterizes much of Jamaica Plain today. I don't know if he would be able to sell a lot of cantaloupes. So let's give him something better suited to today's Jamaica Plain demographic: the Amazon Kindle. It would be interesting to see how he would fare.

"Ebook readers!"

I don't think people would come running. Especially not at $299, $359, or $489 for the various Kindle models. JP may be hip, but its residents work hard for their money.

"Wireless ebook readers with anywhere email!"

Okay, a few people will come out to his truck now. They may well be people who are more interested in "wireless" and "email" than "ebook reader." But a lot of other people will make an assumption about the likely asking price of that wireless service, and that assumption, however mistaken, will keep them from coming out.

As with any street vendor, this gentleman's capacity to survive depends mightily on his ability to embody a basic principle of marketing: he must translate the strengths of his product to a slogan or phrase that will connect with the desires, dreams or fears of his market so that people hear what he is calling out and say to themselves, "I want that. I need that. I cannot do without that. And I can find a way to afford that."

Sooner or later, what the vendor should call out is: "Read and answer email anywhere, anytime on the amazing Amazon Kindle! No monthly charges!"

Then he would get some traffic. (Three Ps: a combination of product, pricing sweet spot, and the power of a strong brand).

"Hey!" you say. "What about truth in advertising?"

Well, what about it? *It's true!*

(*Unless you live outside the U.S., or in one of those sparsely populated areas that does not yet have either of the Sprint wireless services on which the Kindle's wireless features depend).

Email on the Kindle

We can certainly speculate about all kinds of reasons why Amazon has soft-pedaled this information, but the truth is that in addition to being an ebook reader*, the Kindle can be used, right out of the box, to read your email, send replies, and compose outgoing emails.*

The Kindle is not a perfect email device, but it is serviceable, and very handy in a pinch when a laptop or internet connection isn't available.

It's not as multi-featured as sending and receiving email on a notebook or laptop computer, but it's far more portable both in terms of weight and connectivity, since it weighs in at just over 10 ounces (about twice that much for the Kindle DX) and does not need a WiFi signal. You can use it, and be connected to the internet with it, anywhere (*or, at least, anywhere where you could use a Sprint-enabled cellphone): on the beach, in a taxi, or just about anywhere else. In out-of-the-way places where Sprint's fast, broadband EV-DO 3G service is unavailable, there's a good chance you'll be able to connect using Sprint's slower 1xRTT conventional cellular signal. (For a map of the various Kindle wireless coverage areas, see Chapter 16.)

Checking email on the Kindle is noticeably slower than checking email on a smartphone, so you may not want to make too much of this feature if you're one of these CrackBerry types who goes through 1,200 email messages a day. However, it does have two huge advantages over a smartphone.

First, its 6-inch screen is easier on the eyes than a tiny smartphone screen.

Second, let's compare the monthly charges. Smartphone data plans usually begin at around $59.99 a month. The Kindle wireless web service is free to you and me. If you have a calculator on your smartphone, you can easily calculate the difference in price between these two data plans using the formula shown here: $59.99 - $0.00 = $59.99 a month savings, or $719.88 a year (yes, that is more than the price of two Kindle 2s).

(By the way, there is speculation that Amazon won't keep its Whispernet wireless web service free forever. For a detailed discussion of the issues involved, read the chapter of this book entitled Why Your Kindle's Free Wireless Web Browser is a Revolutionary Feature, and Why Amazon Should Keep it Free.)

Okay, so much for comparisons. Let's get down to brass tacks.

Using Mobile Google and Gmail for Kindle Email

The key to using your Kindle device for email is provided by Google. There are other web-based email products that will work, at least sporadically, with the Kindle's web browser, but it is my belief both that Gmail is a superior service and also that Google's commitment to a large and growing suite of mobile products is such that it makes sense for all of us as Kindle owners to engage that product suite and become its patrons and advocates sooner rather than later.

As you may already be aware, Google has designed several applications for use with smartphones, cellphones and, very soon, we hear, the Google phone beta project known as the Android. These products are freely available, and you can see a list of them at the Google Mobile products page. It is quite a list. In addition to the Gmail Google email products, it includes Search, Maps, Calendar, Google Documents, a "411" telephone lookup service, SMS (also known as texting), News, Photos, Reader, Blogger, and Notebook.

If you own a Kindle or are about to own one, and you have any sense of where I'm going with this, I don't blame you if you are beginning to salivate. I'm far from being ready to vouch for the notion that all of these applications work seamlessly with the Kindle. Some of them are a little clunky, and one or two may not be worth using at all on Kindle 1 (with its slower processor). At the very least, they'll take some getting used to. But these web-based software offerings can go a long way toward giving your Kindle the functionality, in a pinch, of an Internet-connected computer. As the Kindle is upgraded in coming generations, this functionality is likely to become more and more powerful.

At first, the idea that you can use the Kindle for email seems a bit surprising. Although Kindle comes with broadband wireless service and a basic, experimental web browser, it is somewhere between risky and impossible for a layman to install third-party software on the device (except for applications that support Kindle commercial partnerships like the one involving Audible.com). Consequently, you could never download or otherwise install email software such as Microsoft Outlook or the old AOL email environment.

That's where Google's mobile applications come in handy. Without the mobile Gmail environment, you could use the Kindle web browser to get to your Gmail account, but navigation and usefulness would be extremely limited. With the mobile Gmail account, it will still be a little slow, but you can handle all the basic tasks involved in working with your email if you follow the steps below:

1. Create a Gmail account if you have not done so already. You will need to do this on your desktop or laptop computer first, by navigating to the Sign Up for Gmail

71

page. Once you have created the account, you should be able to log in to that account on your Kindle without a hitch, but – and this is important – you will have to use the Kindle-compatible URL shown below.

2. Get ready to access your Gmail account on your Kindle by using the 5-way to navigate from the "Home" screen to the "Menu" and then selecting "Experimental." (Make sure your "Wireless" is on before you start). Next, select "Basic Web," then use the 5-way to choose Google from the "My Bookmarks" list that appears automatically on your screen. Google is included in the default listing of Bookmarks that comes fully loaded on the Kindle. You are now in the Mobile Gmail environment. If you prefer to type the GMail URL into your Kindle's web browser directly, use this address:

http://m.gmail.com/

3. The first time you sign in to your Gmail account with your Kindle, you will need to use the Kindle keyboard to type in your Username and Password. After that, Gmail should take you directly to your account most of the time.

4. In your Gmail account, just use the 5-way and the "Next Page" and "Prev Page" bars to move through your Inbox and read your email. It may take you a moment to rid yourself of the urge to scroll down. You can't scroll down, but you can usually accomplish the same thing by pressing the "Next Page" bar.

5. The "Inbox" of your Gmail account will present your most recent messages. Depending on the user-selectable font size you've chosen, you should be able to view 8 or 10 of these message headers at a time so that you can navigate and select easily from your Inbox. Anytime you want to check for brand new messages during a session of working with your Gmail account, just reload the page and your screen will update with any new messages within seconds.

6. If you need to access other areas of your Gmail account such as "Sent Mail," "Drafts," "Contact," or other Gmail features, just use the "Next Page" bar to move toward the end of your Inbox listings. You'll find a listing of choices that probably include "Compose Mail," "Inbox," "Contacts," and "More." Choose the option you need or click on "More" to see further options.

7. Use the "Next Message" and/or "Next Conversation" links, as well as the "Previous" links, rather than trying to scroll up or down, to move serially through your Inbox. The "Next conversation" link will appear at the end of the main body of text of each email message.

8. If you're using "Select" and "Next Page" to navigate among messages in your Inbox, Sent Messages, or any other Gmail label group, you can get back to the listing page by pressing once on the "Back" button or to your main Gmail page by clicking twice. The "Back" button is just below the "Next Page" bar on the right side of the Kindle.

9. To compose and send an email message, follow the process in paragraph 6 above to find "Compose Mail" on your screen, then use the 5-way to choose "Compose Mail." Within seconds you'll see an easy-to-use "Compose Mail" form on your screen. Easy to use in every respect, that is, except for typing with your thumbs.

10. Continue to use the 5-way to choose the "To" box and populate it with one or more email addresses after you choose "Input Field." Then choose "Done." (Actually, one is plenty. You should make sure that you've got this down cold before you start sending out "broadcast" emails).

11. Follow the same process to type in a subject line and the main text of your email. When you're finished, click on the row of buttons directly below the main text input box, then choose "Send." Even if an error message occasionally appears on your screen after you have chosen "Send," your email message has now been sent by Gmail.

You can doublecheck on this, of course, by finding the newly sent message among your "Sent Messages."

12. You can also send replies, add "cc" and "bcc" recipients, and forward messages, using the same basic sequence of steps, by selecting "Reply," "Reply to all," or "Forward" after reading any email message in your Inbox.

13. Once you've mastered the basics of using Gmail on your Kindle, you may want try out some of the other Mobile Google features that we mentioned earlier, such as Google Calendar or the Google Reader. A great daily beginning point for Kindle users who want to get as much as possible from their Kindle web browser is a web "start page" created by Mike Elgan, author of The Book of Kindle blog. Click here to access The Kindle Start Page.

Another feature of the Google environment that can be extremely compatible with some of the more creative uses of your Kindle is called the Gmail Drive. You can use this feature to establish your own partitioned hard drive on the Google servers and access it any time through your Gmail account.

Several of these applications can make your Kindle a far more powerful device than you imagined when you first ordered it. If you can use your Kindle for receiving and sending emails, posting to your blog, maintaining calendar appointments and viewing and editing word files and spreadsheets in the Google Documents application, what exactly is this device you are holding in your hand? An ebook reader? Or a computer?

It is both. It's clearly designed to be an ebook reader, and while a few glitches remain to be ironed out, it rates high in ease of use as an ebook reader. As I've suggested, it's a tad clunky as a computer, but the price, versatility and portability can make up for a lot of clunkiness – and all of a sudden that $359 price tag seems like a bargain.

It will be interesting to see how quickly or flexibly Amazon provides updates or Kindle 2.0 versions to make it easier to use these and other applications. Being a manufacturer was never part of Amazon's DNA, although the Kindle in general is not a bad beginning. It seems far more likely during the next couple of years that Google will alter its mobile applications to accommodate the Kindle than that Amazon will do much to rejigger the Kindle web browser itself. Naturally, there will also be a lot of programming done by creative independent geniuses and other third-party folks.

I should add a note here about the general slowness of using the Kindle for email. Although, as I said, the actual process of navigating among your emails is slower than it is on a laptop, the convenient fact that your broadband service is always there, and comes on with a flip of the switch, helps to offset that lack of speed. You'll never have to sit in a Starbucks for five minutes trying to figure out how to find a hot spot or otherwise connect to a WiFi signal. Matter of fact, you'll never even have to find a Starbucks unless, like me, you are susceptible to getting a Jones for that Starbucks coffee.

Emailing Content to Your Kindle Address

There's one more very cool email-related feature of the Kindle that is well worth mentioning here, in part so that you do not confuse it with the web-based Gmail service that I've been discussing. I recommend, obviously, that you use Gmail for web-based email.

As an entirely separate feature, Amazon also provides your Kindle with its own email address and uses that address to send you any files that you send to Amazon for conversion into Kindle-friendly files. (You first have to approve the email address from which you will be sending any such documents, using the "Manage Your Kindle" page on your Amazon account page, from your computer). In Kindle nomenclature, documents that you send or transfer to your Kindle are called Personal Documents.

Amazon initially announced that it would charge 10 cents per document to email you these Kindle-compatible files, but after going without any charge for over a year began imposing a higher charge: 15 cents per document plus an additional 15 cents for each megabyte of file size, rounded up, after the first megabyte. For this fee, Amazon will convert any document you send in Word, PRC, HTML, TXT, JPEG, GIF, PNG or BMP format. Amazon will also convert PDF files for the Kindle 1 or Kindle 2, whereas the Kindle DX will read PDF files directly if you simply transfer the file via your USB cable from a computer.

Just to be clear, that means you can download the complete file of Moby Dick from Project Gutenberg, send it to your Kindle email account that Amazon has provided, and Amazon will zap it to you as a Kindle document at no charge. (If you're out of wireless range – outside of the applicable Kindle coverage area on the maps to which links are provided in Chapter 16 – you can also send the document to a slightly different form of your Kindle email address [johndoe@free.kindle.com rather than johndoe@kindle.com] and Amazon will send it to your PC so that you can use your USB cable to transfer it to your Kindle).

You can also receive documents that others email to your kindle.com address, but only if you go to your Manage Your Kindle page on your Amazon account and approve the sender in advance.

Using Twitter and Facebook on the Kindle

I connect with Kindle Nation citizens occasionally at Facebook and Twitter, and I've even done so directly from my Kindle at times. You can do the same thing with your Kindle by firing up the Kindle's web Browser and entering one of the mobile addresses, which are http://m.facebook.com and http://m.twitter.com.

Indeed, if you're reading this on your Kindle right now, you can save yourself steps and typing by using the 5-way to click on the mobile Facebook or Twitter address above to go there directly without switching Kindle gears. Once you're there, of course, you will probably find that the 140-character limit for Twitter "tweets" or "status updates" is ideally suited to the keyboard of the Kindle.

Two caveats worth mentioning here:

* As with email, I find it a lot easier to use my Kindle to check and read tweets and Facebook posts than to post them. You can post with your Kindle, but you may find it difficult to determine whether your post has "taken" unless you go back to your profile page to check.

* I also find that the amount of difficulty I have with my Facebook account seems to be intrinsically tied to the number of different devices that I use to log in. Occasionally after accessing Facebook from a friend's computer or other device I find that Facebook sets a higher security hurdle for me the next time I log in via my main computer. Although I understand and appreciate the concern with security, that doesn't mean that it's not a hassle.

Meanwhile, I hope you will connect with me as linked below at Facebook and Twitter:

http://www.facebook.com/stephen.windwalker

http://twitter.com/WindwalkerHere

Troubleshooting Tips if You Have Difficulty Accessing Gmail or Other Web Pages

If you have trouble accessing your Gmail account, another Kindle-compatible webmail account, or any website that is not too graphics-intensive to load onto the Kindle's display, here are a few troubleshooting tips that you may want to try:

* Go to your Kindle web browser "Settings" page (using the menu option from within the browser). Set "View Mode" to Advanced, and select "Enable" for JavaScript.

* It's a good idea every now and then, on that same Settings page, to clear your History and your Cache, which will help protect you against freeze-ups, etc. The trade-off,

which you'll also experience when you reset your Kindle, is that you'll also have to get your thumbs working to type in your user ID and password anew for Gmail and any other websites that require you to log in.

* Just in case your difficulty springs from the URL with which you are entering Gmail, try typing this URL into the URL input field:

m.google.com

or

http://m.google.com

That URL should bring you to a list of the mobile Google products, from which you can select Gmail and be delivered quickly to a Gmail sign-in page.

* Finally – and I'd be more hesitant to suggest the following if I hadn't done this myself more than once – doublecheck your user ID and password for the website on your computer and make sure they work there, just to make sure you haven't changed them and forgotten about the new ones. Then try them again on your pesky Kindle keyboard.

Good luck!

12. Use Kindlepedia for Free Wikipedia Research on Your Kindle

Conventional Wikipedia Research on the Kindle

I can't imagine a single Kindle owner anywhere in the world who is not already familiar with Wikipedia, the online crowd-sourced encyclopedia with over 13 million collaboratively written articles. In addition to the fact that it is the seventh most popular website in the world according to Alexa.com's traffic rankings, Wikipedia is a very high-profile part of the Kindle experience already, since it's featured as a prominent channel for any user-initiated Kindle search along with Google, the Kindle Store, the Kindle's onboard dictionary and its library of ebooks and other documents.

The opportunity for readers to move quickly and easily – using the Kindle's absolutely free wireless 3G web browser – between content on their Kindles and the kind of supplemental references and information that they will find on Wikipedia is bound to enrich the educational usefulness of the Kindle, and not just for college students. My 11-year-old son moves seamlessly between his life and Wikipedia explanations of the few remaining things he doesn't understand, and I'm learning more slowly to do the same. By leaving the door constantly cracked between any content that we're reading and Wikipedia's rich universe of information and content, the Kindle offers astonishing potential for us to place the words that we read in the kinds of textured historical and cultural contexts that make them more vivid than they could ever be in a traditional book, no matter how much we may love print on paper.

But Wikipedia is more than just a place to visit for a few seconds here and there in the margins of one's reading experiences. The extensive content to be found there is worthy of reading time all its own, and offers inquisitive readers an opportunity to move organically – or whimsically, for that matter – across dozens or hundreds or thousands of "articles" in ways that allow the construction of remarkable aedifices of personal knowledge and contextual understanding. Thomas Wolfe may have arrived at Harvard in 1920 with the dream of reading every volume in the university's Harry Elkins Widener Library, but I cannot help but think that he might have enjoyed his self-education more, begun it earlier, and avoided the constant need to wash the dust from his hands if his times had allowed him access to a Kindle with an always-on Wikipedia connection.

There is more than one way to get to Wikipedia on the Kindle, and here are several:

* Since Wikipedia is a website that you have probably visited many times already on your computer, it might seem that the best way to get there is to open the Kindle's Experimental Web Browser and use the Wikipedia bookmark that Amazon has placed there. No. That route will take much longer and may well deliver you to a huge, slow-to-load Wikipedia main page on which navigation and the mere entry of a search term will be slower than molasses, so slow that it may freeze your Kindle by overloading its native (RAM) memory.

* Instead, just type any word or phrase which you might want to research on Wikipedia, and move the 5-way controller to the right to select "wikipedia" and begin a much speedier search.

* If you prefer to search beyond Wikipedia and see what you can find in your Kindle content, in your Kindle's dictionary, and on the web, follow the same process without the "@wiki" prefix. (You don't need to turn on your wireless switch if you are interested only in listings that are already on your Kindle or in your Kindle dictionary.) Your Kindle screen will give you a choice of places to find the word or term. Just click on any of the alternatives and you'll be taken there.

But now there's more, thanks to a new Kindle app called Kindlepedia.

Wire Up and Tag Kindlepedia to Educate Yourself Any Time on Any Topic

First, a tip of the hat to Edukindle creator Will DeLamater and Kindle Formatting author Joshua Tallent for creating the Kindlepedia tool discussed here, to Kindle Chronicles podcaster Len Edgerly for bringing it to my attention by featuring it on his program, and to old friend, author, teacher, fellow traveler and classmate of Len's and mine Ned Stuckey-French for getting my thoughts percolating about the pedagogical possibilities here.

DeLamater and Tallent have collaborated on an extremely useful and elegant new application that allows Kindle readers to create a Kindle "book" within a few seconds from any Wikipedia listing and transfer (download) it to a Kindle either via USB or Whispernet for offline reading and research at one's leisure. Not surprisingly, given Joshua's virtuosity with Kindle formatting issues, the resulting Wikipedia-based "book" arrives on a Kindle in a nicely formatted, easy-to-read state, with external web links intact so that one is never more than a click away from extending one's research even further, including references beyond Wikipedia. Here are the steps, and just for fun I'll use the Wikipedia article on one of my favorite underappreciated baseball players of the past century, Bernie Carbo:

> * On your computer, go to the Kindlepedia page on the Edukindle website at http://bit.ly/Kindlepedia. (No need to try to do this Kindlepedia procedure directly from your Kindle; I've already tried and it doesn't work).

> * Type in the URL of the Wikipedia entry that you wish to make into a Kindle "book" in the entry field in the center of the screen. If you are relatively certain that a brief keyword or phrase will produce the desired article, you can try that:

Enter a Wikipedia URL here: | Bernie Carbo | | Create Kindle Book |

for example: http://en.wikipedia.org/wiki/Martin_luther_king

* Click on the "Create Kindle Book" button, and within a few seconds you'll see a new screen with these buttons in the center of the display:

Download Bernie_Carbo.mobi

⇐ Create another book

* Click on the "download" button from your computer's dialogue box (or a quick file search, for, in this case "Bernie_Carbo.mobi") and note the location where the downloaded file is being saved on your computer.

* Transfer this "Bernie_Carbo.mobi" file to your Kindle either by sending it as an attachment to your @kindle.com email address (in which case Amazon will charge you 15 cents per megabyte rounded up and send the converted file to your Kindle via Whispernet) or, for free, by connecting your Kindle to your computer via USB, copying the saved file from your computer to the "documents" folder in your Kindle's main directory via Finder, My Computer, or whatever file management program you use with your computer, and using the "Eject" Kindle command to disconnect the Kindle from your computer.

You should now find the Kindle-formatted "Bernie Carbo" book at the top of your Kindle's Home screen if your Home display is organized to show all documents, most recent first:

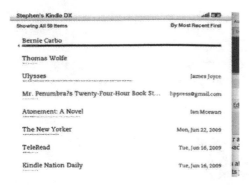

As with any other Kindle book, click on "Bernie Carbo" and begin reading or let your Kindle read the content aloud to you. While reading, you'll be able to click on any live web link such as the Baseball-Reference link shown here:

- Pinch hitter
- 1975 World Series
- The Sporting News Rookie of the Year Award
- Career statistics and player information from Baseball-Reference
- The Sporting News (article)
- Baseball's 25 Greatest Moments

to extend your research to, say, viewing Carbo's lifetime stats:

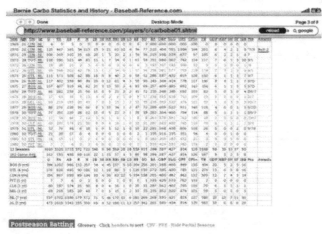

Okay, if you are thinking that this great new research tool is going to curse you with an unmanageably long list or catalog of "books" on your Kindle, here's a useful tip from a March 9, 2009 Kindle Nation piece (which referenced a Kindle Chronicles podcast from March 6) on *A Brilliant Way To Apply Tags To Organize Your Kindle Content*:

Amazon's failure to provide user-defined content management folders or labels is one of the major disappointments offsetting the many improvements that we have seen with the Kindle 2 [and Kindle DX], but a Kindle owner named Larry Goss has developed an elegant work-around system that allows him to "tag" any title on his Kindle. To hear his approach, check out the March 6 edition of Len Edgerly's Kindle Chronicles podcast. Larry's idea is detailed in the show comments section a little over two-thirds of the way into the podcast. The gist of it is that you can use any Kindle's annotation feature to "tag" your content by genre, status, or any other qualifier as long as you create "words" that would not otherwise be found in your documents. For example, I might create two tags for science fiction novels on my Kindle, and thus annotate the first page of each either with SWSCIFIREAD or SWSCIFINEW, to signify Stephen Windwalker's science fiction novels read or unread. Once the annotation is saved, books with a particular tag will display in the search results whenever you enter that tag. Yes, it is a work-around, but I hope you will agree that it is brilliant in its workable simplicity, and join me in thanking Larry and Len.

For my purposes, I just create a tag at the beginning of each of these Wikipedia-based books. The first four letters are always "SWKP" for "Stephen Windwalker Kindlepedia" and subsequent letters are the briefest and most simple tag for the content, so that for the Carbo content, I simply open the file on my Kindle, choose "Add a Note or Highlight" from the Menu, type in "swkp carbo," and click on "save note" at the bottom of the dialogue box. Then I will find the content anytime by typing in "SWKP CARBO," whereas typing in "SWKP" will show me all my Wikipedia-based content and typing in "CARBO" will show me all Carbo references on my Kindle. Fortunately, if I forget some of my

own tags, I can also access them by opening the "My Clippings"
file on my Home screen.

13. The Myth of the Kindle's "Standard" $9.99 Price and the ABCs of Kindle Store Pricing

If you were to rely strictly on the mainstream media coverage of the Kindle for your information, you could not be faulted for believing that most Kindle books are priced at $9.99.

In fact, only one out of ever seven Kindle books – 13.9% as of July 28, 2009 – is priced at $9.99. The vast majority of the rest – 58% of all Kindle editions – are priced below $9.99, including over 30,000 titles that are priced anywhere from 99 cents down to "Free:"

KINDLE STORE BOOKS CATALOG BY PRICE, July 28, 2009

PRICE RANGE	NUMBER OF TITLES	PERCENTAGE OF TOTAL LISTINGS	NUMBER OF CUSTOMER REVIEWS	REPRESENTATION IN TOP 100 KINDLE STORE BESTSELLERS
$0.00	7,416	2.28%	1,003	32
$0.01 to $0.98	3,115	0.96%	502	0
$0.99	20,243	6.22%	3,078	0
$1.00	7,105	2.18%	1,056	0
$1.01 to $2.99	35,696	10.97%	5,600	0
$3.00 to $4.99	59,064	18.14%	12,509	0
$5.00 to $7.49	33,318	10.24%	15,530	5
$7.50 to $9.98	23,028	7.07%	13,374	15
$9.99	45,375	13.94%	35,314	40
$10.00 to $14.99	10,266	3.15%	6,504	6
$15.00 to $19.99	11,247	3.46%	5,933	2
$20.00 to $29.99	6,007	1.85%	2,788	0
$30.00 to $39.99	14,191	4.36%	4,655	0
$40.00 to $49.99	6,694	2.06%	2,127	0
$50.00 to $99.99	21,681	6.66%	4,660	0
$100.00 to $199.99	19,022	5.84%	2,166	0
$200.00 to $999.99	2,019	0.62%	149	0
$1000.00 to 6431.20	32	0.01%	2	0
TOTAL	325,519	100.00%	116,950	100

Part of the cause of this confusion comes from Amazon itself, since the company's marketing efforts for the Kindle have sometimes focused on the $9.99 price point as if it were a standard price.

However, Amazon deserves credit for making it easy for its Kindle customers to find free and low-priced books in the Kindle Store. As Kindle spokesperson Cynthia Portugal told the Associated Press for an August 2009 article on the popularity of free books in the Kindle Store: "We work hard to provide customers with the best value possible and pass savings on to them whenever possible." Amazon includes free titles in its bestselling sales rankings because, Portugal said, the list is "based on customer orders — customers are still ordering these books, they just have a price tag of $0.00."

In any case, it's reasonable to expect that pricing issues will continue to work themselves out in the Kindle Store, based on several market forces:

* Competition from other eBook platforms. If another platform emerges with some popularity and market share, it could undercut Kindle Store prices and bring influence to bear on them.

* Pressure by Kindle owners. For instance, the $9.99 Kindle Store price boycott gathered some momentum in 2009 as Kindle owners steered business away from books priced over $9.99. See http://bit.ly/999KindlePriceBoycott.

* Publishing industry economics, as the ebook share of the total reading market increases. Many publishers still see ebooks as icing on the cake of traditional print-on-paper profits. But if ebooks come to surpass print book sales, those same publishers will require ebooks to carry a proportionate share of the basic editorial, marketing, creative, and pre-press costs now supported by print books. On the other hand, the natural downward spiral of pricing for online content and the fact that ebooks don't carry production, warehousing, or fulfillment costs should keep ebook prices from reaching current print-book levels such as $30 to $35 for the latest Dan Brown or Stephen King novel.

It's one of the more telling signs of the infancy of the ebook sector of the publishing industry that, so far, the Kindle has not faced serious tipping-point competition either in hardware or in content. As this competition emerges, it will have an impact on both of these aspects of Kindle pricing.

If you're a subscriber to Kindle Nation, or if you're reading this book, chances are good that you're both a savvy shopper and an avid reader who is interested in getting good content at a great price whenever it is available. Personally, I make a serious effort to balance my interests as a reader and Kindle owner, as a strong advocate for Kindle owners, and as an author and publisher. I believe it's important for all of us to support pricing that keeps writers writing, publishers publishing, readers reading, and Amazon selling all kinds of reading content, and I hope you'll share my interest in this balance.

If you want to have an impact on prices in the Kindle Store, I recommend that you consider three approaches:

* Read the article on the $9.99 Kindle Price Boycott and find more links at http://bit.ly/999KindlePriceBoycott, and consider participating.

* Write brief but thoughtful reviews of Kindle editions on the Amazon.com website to help guide your fellow Kindle owners to quality.

* Sign up for Kindle Store price alerts at Zoo Alert so that you can time your Kindle book purchases to get the best prices.

14. The Politics of "Free" Books
In the Age of the Kindle

Let's keep this brief. It's certainly neither my assumption nor my expectation that you are here out of interest in the politics of the ebook industry or "movement." But if you are an avid reader, you are likely to be affected by these issues in one way or another. But rather than go on at too great length about these issues myself, I'll suggest a few very basic definitions and point in the direction of some material that I believe would be helpful for those who wish to read further.

When people talk about "free" digital contant such as ebooks, digital music files, and video content, they are usually speaking of one or both of two kinds of "free," either:

* Content that is free of charge, zero-priced, or available for the taking through a legal download or other transaction; or

* Content that is free of digital restrictions, such as the Digital Rights Management (DRM) restrictions placed on many Kindle books by Amazon, which might limit one from making various non-commercial uses of that content.

Zero-Priced Content

The chapters you've been reading in this ebook have been all about various entirely legal ways of acquiring content at zero price, and we've already seen how free books have come increasingly to dominate the top Kindle Store bestsellers. When books are free, the content is free because either:

* it's no longer protected by copyright due to its publication date, and is therefore in the "public domain,"

* it has been explicitly released to the public domain through a Creative Commons license or some similar device, or

* its price has been set at free or zero either temporarily or permanently by its author, publisher, or retailer in order to make it more widely available, as a promotional strategy for itself or other works, as a "loss leader," or in order to generate ancillary revenue with an alternative model in which the content drives traffic, affiliate fees, or advertising revenue.

Issues related to free ebooks, music, and newspaper content have exploded over the past two decades with the explosive growth in popularity of the web. *The Long Tail* author Chris Anderson has been a leading herald of a downward price spiral toward free content, most recently in his book *Free: The Future of a Radical Price*, which at this writing is ranked #19 in the Kindle Store as a free Kindle edition and #836 in the main Amazon bookstore as a $26.99 hardcover.

Whether this "downward price spiral toward free content" is seen as a viral marketing strategy or as the inevitable consequence of the spread of new technologies, it's obviously unsustainable at its final, absolute level. Whether one thinks of Anderson or me or anyone else who writes a book entitled *Free* as authors, as content providers, or as search engine and advertising magnets, either we must have ways of being paid for our work or we will have to find other work. Author Malcolm Gladwell has offered an uneven critique of the free content approach in his New Yorker review of Anderson's book at http://bit.ly/Gladwell-on-Free.

While controversies over the apparent death spiral of a newsprint-based newspaper industry and the rise, fall, and rise of Napster and various business ventures which followed it have made us all a little more knowledgeable and a lot more opinionated about free content and its attendant issues, it's important to remember that there are special issues in each category there that should keep us from lumping all forms of free content together. With some exceptions, ebooks don't suffer because they contain information that readers would otherwise get for free online, as occurs with various sources of news, and with even fewer exceptions, ebooks can't be seen as loss leaders to inspire readers to buy concert tickets for the next live show by Stephenie Meyer or James Patterson, to reach for analogy based on the current revenue structure of much of the music industry.

DRM and DRM-Free Content

I discussed Digital Rights Management (DRM) briefly in the context of digital music such as MP3 files in Chapter 10, but it is an equally gnarly issue in the context of the Kindle specifically and ebooks in general. The much-ballyhooed and often confused July 2009 "the Kindle ate my homework" controversy over Amazon's removal of two copyright-violating George Orwell novels from customers' Kindles shined a light on our worst fears about DRM.

Amazon's motivation for its DRM policy may well be based on a business need to protect publishers' copyright interests as a necessary basis for their participating, but one does not need to sport a tinfoil hat to realize that DRM can become a more ominous restriction in a world where the Kindle's Whispernet wireless connectivity is a two-way street. In essence, the fact that most Kindle editions currently come with DRM, combined with Amazon's nearly constant wireless access to our Kindle hardware, gave Amazon the power to go back into our Kindles to grab and delete not only the books that customers had purchased and downloaded, but also the annotations, highlights, and highlights that they had made in the text.

To the shock and outrage of many, that is just the "Orwellian" step that Amazon took when it discovered that two of the Orwell novels being offered in the Kindle Store were in copyright violation. Even for those of us who understand and sympathize with the importance of protecting the Orwell copyright interest, there seemed little excuse for the fact that Amazon acted surreptitiously, without warning, and without providing customers with the chance to download an alternative copyright-compliant version and synch up annotations.

To his credit, Amazon founder and CEO Jeff Bezos offered an exemplary apology for the company's actions. That hasn't kept some customers from filing or contemplating class action lawsuits over the matter. It will continue to fester as part of a broader set of concerns around DRM until, at the very least, Amazon brings greater clarity to the DRM issue and guarantees that it won't repeat such actions in the future.

I believe it is likely that Amazon will eventually follow in the footsteps of Apple, iTunes, and the iPod with respect to DRM by loosening DRM restrictions on Kindle editions in the future, perhaps at a pricing premium. But such predictions from me fall far short of a guarantee, and as technology blogger Mike Elgan pointed out in an interview with Len Edgerly on The Kindle Chronicles 53, DRM is very much in Amazon's business interest now in exactly the same way it was, at first, in Apple's interest, because "the biggest buyers of books actually invest their time and money into a format which is Amazon's format:"

> The way [Apple] set up the iTunes store and the way they did DRM and all that stuff.... After a year or two went by and Apple became the number one player people had invested enormous amounts of money in buying songs, and to move to a competitive player was kind of out of the question for a lot of people because they couldn't just abandon a thousand dollars worth of investment in songs.... [So, since] the top five per cent of book buyers buy 20 per cent of the books ... the biggest buyers of books ... those heavy duty users .. those are the people who Amazon has essentially captured into its format [with the Kindle].

The reality, of course, is that we'll have to wait and see. The practices and initiatives of readers, authors, publishers, retailers and perhaps even courts and government agencies will play out in ways that are probably too complex to predict at the present time. Even Amazon itself will have to share the tiller as we navigate these rapids. Meanwhile, for an excellent introduction to DRM issues as they relate to ebooks, I recommend DRM: A TeleRead Primer, posted on December 6, 2008 by Chris Meadows at http://www.teleread.org/2008/12/06/drm-a-teleread-primer/.

15. Why Your Kindle's Free Wireless Web Browser is a Revolutionary Feature, and Why Amazon Should Keep it Free

The service that Amazon calls Whispernet is actually a 3G EVDO wireless broadband service that enables the Kindle to connect to Sprint's U.S. wireless data network. This service, the same on the Kindle 2 and Kindle DX as on the original Kindle, is available in most densely populated areas, but not everywhere. If your Kindle is within Sprint's United States wireless data network, you won't need a WiFi connection, a computer connection, or any synchronization steps.

The process of ordering a book from the Kindle Store and then seeing it on your Kindle display is only slightly slower than the speed of thought. Of course, if you're outside the network coverage area, the Kindle also comes with a USB cable for easy connection to your desktop or laptop computer. You always have the option of having Amazon send any Kindle content to your computer so that you can transfer it to your computer via USB cable.

When the original Kindle was launched in November 2007, the device's Whispernet-enabled "Basic Web" feature was designated as "experimental," which meant that it could be discontinued by Amazon at any time. There was considerable speculation on Kindle owners' message boards and elsewhere that the web connectivity would eventually be considered too expensive by Amazon and discontinued. However, the service is a popular feature with many Kindle owners, whether one considers it ancillary or essential to the device's connectivity with the Kindle Store. The store, of course, is the key commercial portal through which the Kindle connects our wallets and credit cards to Amazon's corporate bank accounts. And from our point of view as readers and book buyers, it's the portal through which Amazon is able to dazzle us with nearly instantaneous delivery of the books and other content that we want to read on our Kindles.

Although the Kindle has been marketed initially as an "ebook reader," its array of features actually sets the bar considerably higher than any of its predecessor ebook devices. Electronic reading devices have been around for decades, but until the launch of the Kindle they failed to gain any serious traction.

These ancillary Kindle features include audio, graphic, and even game-playing capacities, but foremost among them is the Kindle's free broadband wireless connectivity (via the Sprint 3G EV-DO service), which has significant benefits for the device's functionality both with ebooks and with other content. Such a data connection ordinarily costs over $50 to $75 per month, but Amazon pays the entire bill (whatever it is), handles any problems with Sprint, and uses the connection to run a "Whispernet" service that allows Kindle owners to download content – books, newspapers, magazines, and blogs – within seconds of purchasing it from the Kindle Store.

One of the more intriguing aspects of the Kindle's initial rollout in November 2007 was the degree to which Jeff Bezos and Amazon played the Kindle's most revolutionary feature so close to the vest. By marketing the Kindle as an ebook reader, Amazon kept the public focus away from the Kindle's stunning EV-DO wireless connectivity.

Why stunning?

Five main reasons:

* It allows seamless, simple same-minute delivery of any content purchased in the Kindle Store.

* It transforms the Kindle into a web-browsing computer that can access nearly any website.

* It is fast – essentially broadband over a cellular network – although the speed of the connection itself is unfortunately brought low by the Kindle's slow processing speed.

* It is free, as compared with the $40 to $90 per month that you would pay to connect an iPhone,

Blackberry or any other device to EV-DO or other wireless data services.

* The service is ubiquitous in well-populated areas, so that you never have to search for a WiFi hot spot. (Indeed, if the Kindle's popularity continues to grow, it could do serious harm to Starbucks). (For a map of the various Kindle wireless coverage areas, see Chapter 16).

So, did you get this? Did I just tell you that you could buy a mobile computer for $199 to $489 with all of the above features, and never pay a dime to connect to the web?

Almost. That "never" remains in play, but we'll come back to that.

First, let's just take pains to make this clear: the wireless connectivity, combined with the fact that the Kindle comes with its own built-in "Basic Web" browser, means that calling the Kindle an ebook reader is like calling the iPhone a cordless telephone. The Kindle is a potentially revolutionary convergence device.

To consider just how revolutionary and disruptive the Kindle could become, we should compare it briefly to three other convergence devices: the Blackberry, the iPhone and the laptop or notebook computer.

At 10.3 ounces in a package slightly smaller than a thin trade paperback, the Kindle 1 and 2 is a little bit larger and more cumbersome than the Blackberry or the iPhone. But compared with a laptop, there is no contest. You don't need a backpack, a book bag or a briefcase to carry a Kindle. It is exactly the same as carrying a lightweight paperback book. While the Kindle DX weighs about twice as much, it still compares favorably with a laptop or netbook computer.

Both the Blackberry and the iPhone allow many people to leave their laptops at home when they leave their homes or offices. But it's a bit of a toss-up. You could go either way.

But if I am carrying a Kindle when I leave my house in the morning, I cannot imagine why I would ever want to carry a laptop. Even in its small, lightweight package, the Kindle's 6-inch screen is about 3 times the size of the screens on the iPhone or other smartphones, and much easier on the eyes. If I carry a laptop, either I have to look for a WiFi hotspot or I have to pay $59.99 to $89.99 a month for 3G wireless service.

Case closed. Or open, if it's a Kindle case.

The biggest disadvantage for the Kindle, of course, is that it's not a cell phone (or is that an advantage?). It also does not make coffee. (Of course, if the Kindle 2.0 happens to show up with the capacity to connect to Skype VOIP service with that wireless connectivity – something that I acknowledge is quite unlikely – then all bets are off).

It's interesting to speculate about why Amazon effectively did a soft launch of the free wireless "Basic Web" service while simultaneously doing a well-hyped, cover-of-Newsweek, get-Jeff-on-Charlie-Rose hard launch of the Kindle as an ebook reader. Several possible reasons come to mind:

* the desire to focus on the book-reading experience for book-reading purists who might be scared off by the potential distractions of web and web-based email connectivity

* a business need to downplay and undervalue the impact and worth of Amazon's EV-DO contract with Sprint

* business competition or regulatory issues too arcane to break down here

* the possibility that Amazon will decide at some future time to begin charging for the "Basic Web" wireless service

While a couple of these issues might be reaching a bit, each of them is interesting in its own way. Let's focus here on the issue that will have the most traction for current and future Kindle owners: the prospect that Amazon might begin assessing a monthly service fee for the wireless web. In the early blog and user-group discussions about the Kindle, there has been significant attention paid to this prospect.

It has not been lost on Kindle's early adopter users that, in its Amazon Kindle: License Agreement and Terms of Use, Amazon expressly provides for such a service fee:

> Amazon provides wireless connectivity free of charge to you for certain content shopping and downloading services on your Device. You may be charged a fee for wireless connectivity for your use of other wireless services on your Device, such as Web browsing and downloading of personal files, should you elect to use those services. We will maintain a list of current fees for such services in the Kindle Store. Amazon reserves the right to discontinue wireless connectivity at any time or to otherwise change the terms for wireless connectivity at any time, including, but not limited to (a) limiting the number and size of data files that may be transferred using wireless connectivity and (b) changing the amount and terms applicable for wireless connectivity charges. (February 2009 version current as of August 1, 2009).

Does that cinch it? Perhaps. Perhaps not.

The wireless service obviously has significant value. If Amazon made the service a user option with a service charge of, say, $12.95 a month, many users would pay the fee for the opportunity to use the web from nearly anywhere with such a portable, lightweight, easy-to-read device. Many others would opt out, to the fallback of using their Kindle for reading and visiting the Kindle Store – sort of like using a Maserati as a student-driver car.

Amazon could charge for the Basic Web wireless, and there are plenty of people who believe they will, simply because they can. After all, there is no business model more popular on the Web than the perpetual monthly service charge. Compared to the wheelbarrows full of cash that Amazon will generate by selling the Kindle itself, a Kindle monthly wireless charge could generate truckloads.

Far be it from me to offer business advice to Jeff Bezos, but if Jeff calls and asks my advice, I will suggest a nominal fee of, say, $2.99 a month for the Basic Web wireless connectivity, because I think that a fee at that level would actually highlight the value of the service and inspire more people to check it out and use it. After all, we all deem ourselves worthy of premium-level service, don't we? All the better if we can actually afford it.

In addition to the nominal fee, it might make sense for Amazon to add on a further per-gigabyte transfer fee for individuals or business users whose usage exceeds some basic level. (One would expect that Amazon proxies all wireless traffic with the Kindle as a condition of its contract with Sprint, and thus could easily and seamlessly measure and bill for an individual's usage volume).

Why would it be a mistake for Amazon to charge too high a rate for Basic Web wireless service? Amazon understands the concept of loss leaders better than any other business in the world (see http://en.wikipedia.org/wiki/Loss_leader for a straightforward explanation of this marketing concept). By pricing customers out of wireless wbe service, Amazon would risk no longer:

*** *Maximizing Kindle Unit Sales*.** Despite the fact that Amazon has downplayed the Basic Web wireless service, the service is and will continue to be a major motivating factor behind sales of the Kindle. It will still be a major motivating factor at $2.99 a month. At $19.95 a month, not so much.

*** *Maximizing Kindle User Time*.** The more that the Kindle works as a convergence device, the more its owners will use it rather than other devices. The more Kindle owners use their Kindles as computers, the more they'll buy from Amazon. (The importance of this issue, of course, would be far greater if rather than just being able to shop the Kindle Store, Kindle owners were able to shop the entire Amazon store from their Kindles).

Maximizing Kindle Book Sales. The more Kindle users are on their Kindles, the more Kindle books, newspapers and articles like this one they'll buy. Since it's clear that Kindle buyers are self-identified active readers, it's likely that many or most of them could soon be buying a Kindle book per week, which would generate more revenue for Amazon than monthly services fees.

Maximizing Other Amazon Sales. It obviously benefits Amazon to make it easy and seamless for Kindle Store browsing to be linked heavily, and "sticky" with, general Amazon store browsing. Naturally, that will mean that Kindle owners who are constantly on their Kindles because of the device's versatility will not only be the best Kindle Store customers. They will also be among the best Amazon store customers for music, video, software and hardware, and all the other countless merchandise departments at Amazon.com.

Heading Off Convergence Device Competition. As greater numbers of people realize the numerous ways they can use a Kindle, its greatest competition will come from the iPhone and the iPod Touch, the Blackberry, the Google phone, and laptops and handheld computers. This competition will be the primary technology competition of the remaining years of this decade. The longer Amazon keeps the Kindle wireless web free, the greater its ultimate market share. Amazon, the subject of Robert Spector's book, *Amazon.com: Get Big Fast*, also understands the importance of dominating market share better than any business in the world. While some of these potential competitor devices may allow the device owners to read books with them, Whispernet makes the Kindle the only ereader that offers instantaneous content delivery of over 350,000 titles.

Building the Customer Experience. Bezos has built Amazon around the idea that profit and customer loyalty follow naturally when you provide an unparalleled customer experience in selection, price and service. Keeping the wireless service free or cheap will be a huge boost to the customer experience during the next five years, as the Kindle Book inventory grows toward Bezos' ultimate vision of including every book ever printed. Amazon's market position with respect both to ereader devices and content would only benefit. Conversely, many customers would see a move to milk revenue from the service as a bait-and-switch tactic, despite the fact that Amazon has already suggested such a move in its small print.

Stay tuned. As is so often true with Amazon, it will be interesting to see what's next. And if you have an opinion about what Amazon should do with the web browser or any other services, the Kindle team wants to hear from you. Make democracy work in the land of the Kindle by emailing your feedback to kindle-feedback@amazon.com.

16. Tips for Making the Most of Your Kindle's Free Features

a. Check Sprint's Wireless Coverage for Your Kindle

Checking Sprint Wireless Coverage for the Kindle 1

Just to compare notes on the relative strength of the Sprint wireless coverage signal for the Kindle 2 as compared with the Kindle 1, you may want to navigate first to view the Kindle 1 map at

http://www.showmycoverage.com/IMPACT.jsp

and enter zip codes or other information to see mapping of Sprint wireless coverage areas anywhere in the United States. To find Internet coverage while you're traveling inside or outside the U.S., www.jiwire.com is a helpful resource.

Checking Sprint Wireless Coverage for the Kindle 2 or the Kindle DX

For the Kindle 2 map, just navigate to

http://www.showmycoverage.com/mycoverage.jsp?id=A102ZON

and enter zip codes or other information to see mapping of Sprint wireless coverage areas for the Kindle 2 anywhere in the United States. To find Internet coverage while you are traveling inside or outside the U.S., www.jiwire.com is a helpful resource.

As you can see by comparing the Kindle 2 Whispernet coverage area with the coverage area for the Kindle 1, the area has been greatly expanded for the Kindle 2 and Kindle DX, due mainly to more powerful connectivity built into the unit itself.

b. Free for You: How to Ask for and Use a Kindle Gift Certificate

Whether you're a student contemplating Kindle textbook purchases or just a happy Kindle owner of any age who is blessed with loved ones who want to feed your need to read, there's more than one route to "free" with the Kindle. If you have family or friends who want to supplement your Kindle reading budget, the easiest way for them to help out is to send you a Kindle Gift Certificate, either electronically or by snail mail.

Early in 2009 Amazon rolled out a new Kindle Gift Card, which makes it a snap to provide Kindle owners with funds for all those Kindle books (and other content) they want to read and buy on their Kindles. This newly introduced Kindle Gift Card is available in any amount from $5 to $5,000 and addresses a pet peeve of Kindle owners and their friends and loved ones, which is that – unlike everything else on the virtual shelves of the Amazon store – there was no smooth and easy way to make gifts of Kindle content.

To ask for a Kindle gift card as a gift, just email the Kindle Gift Card link from A Kindle Home Page to the person you're asking. If they are having Amazon send the gift card to you electronically, make sure that you send the link from the email account that is associated with your main Amazon account. They should use that same email account – and **not** your you@kindle.com email address! – as the recipient account.

To order a Kindle gift card, gift certificate, or email a gift credit in any quantity or any amount from $5 to $5,000, just click on the link mentioned above, look for the "click to select design" link, and use the "Select" button to choose the "Amazon Kindle" gift card. Complete your purchase and you're all set, and yes, you can even send a Kindle gift card to yourself as a way of streamlining your Kindle purchases or, perish the thought, staying on a budget!

Here's the drill straight from Kindle Support on how to use these forms of Amazon currency with a Kindle:

If you've redeemed an Amazon Gift Card, Gift Certificate, or Promotional Certificate to your Amazon.com account, any available balance will be used for your Kindle Store purchase before your credit or debit card is charged. Your Amazon.com account must list a valid 1-Click payment method even if you intend to pay for your purchase with a Gift Card balance. Your Gift Card balance cannot be used to pay for subscription content from the Kindle Store.

To redeem a Gift Card to Your Account:

1. Visit http://www.amazon.com/gp/youraccount.

2. Click "Apply a gift card to your account."

3. Sign in with your email address and password.

4. Enter your claim code and click "Redeem now." Your funds will automatically be applied to your next order.

Please note: The "Amazon Kindle" designation for the gift card described in this chapter is strictly, at present, a design designation, which you select by selecting the Kindle design from the choices offered on the Amazon website. These gift cards may be used anywhere in the Amazon Store.

c. A Directory of Kindle-Friendly Web Links

The following list of web links is offered to help you make the most of the Kindle's free wireless web browser. Many of the Kindle-compatible links and bookmarks in this section were the work of Kindle owner, reader, and incredibly competent and helpful person extraordinaire **Adrienne Cousins**. I am grateful for her willingness to allow me to make them part of this book for Kindle 2 owners. We have done our best to provide up-to-date links, but please note both that web addresses occasionally become obsolete and that some links may work poorly with your Kindle for any of several possible reasons that are outside our control.

Please feel free to share this list of links with others. I've added some additional pages to the list, and some of this material is also available online on a single web page at A Kindle Home Page.

This section is a collection of links to mobile web sites, blogs and RSS feeds, displayed in a concise format for the Kindle screen. Many of these links utilize an app called Skweezer. Links are organized by topic. While some of these links have a regional bias, our hope is that they will give you some ideas about connections that you can make with your Kindle if you live in a different part of the country. Plus you are always welcome in New England!

Clicking on a link with your Kindle 2 5-way will open that site in the Kindle browser. Pressing the BACK button will return you to this book at the same page you left.

Once you visit a website to which you expect to return often, bookmark it on your Kindle. (But use discretion, or your list of Kindle web bookmarks could get so long that it becomes inefficient).

To bookmark any of these websites in your Kindle 2 web browser, once the page loads onto your Kindle screen, just press "Menu" and use the 5-way to select and click on "Bookmark This Page."

One important tip for using most of the web features that you'll find in this book: many of them depend upon you changing two settings on the "Basic Web Settings" display screen on your Kindle 2:

- To reach the "Basic Web Settings" display screen, press the "Menu" button while you're in the Kindle 2 web browser mode, and select "Settings" with the 5-way.

- When you arrive at the Settings page, make sure that your Kindle 2 is set to "Advanced Mode" on the top line of this screen, and to "Enable Javascript."

- If you don't anticipate using images as you make use of the Kindle 2 web browser, you can speed up its capacity to process content by selecting "Disable Images" on the bottom line of this display screen.

Since these settings are all "toggle" settings, a hasty look at this web settings screen can be a bit confusing. When you conform your Kindle 2 web browser to the settings I've just described, your web settings screen will read as follows from top to bottom:

Settings

Switch to Basic Mode
Clear Cache
Clear History
Clear Cookies
Disable Javascript
Always disabled in Basic Mode
Enable images

If you aren't already in the web browser mode, you can get there by pressing the Home button followed by the Menu button and selecting "Experimental" and "Basic Web." You can also get to the Web by beginning to type a word or phrase from within any document, pushing the 5-way all the way to the right twice when a search field is displayed, and selecting "Google" or "Wikipedia" as your search medium.

INDEX TO LINKS

Kindle Store, App, and Kindle Essential Links
Freebies for Your Kindle
Amazon Store Bestseller Links
Best Blogs
Blog Lists
Book Catalogs
Book Reviews
Business & Finance
Comics
eBook Downloads, Support & Discussions

Entertainment
Hobbies
Kindle Blogs
Kindle Gear
Magazines
Mail & Message
Mobile RSS Readers
Mobile Transcoders
Mobile Site Lists
Newspapers
News: National
News: Sports
News: Technology
Reference
Shipping Carriers
Shopping
Travel
Weather

Glossary

Kindle Store, App, and Kindle Essential Links

Kindle Support
Kindle Support Phone Number *1-866-321-8851*

FREE:
How to Get Millions of Free Books, Songs, Podcasts, Periodicals &
Free eMail, Facebook, Twitter and Wireless Web With Your
Amazon Kindle, Kindle 2, Kindle DX,
Or Kindle for iPhone app
By Stephen Windwalker of Kindle Nation Daily

http://bit.ly/FreeKindleStoreBooks
http://bit.ly/FreeKindlePromotionalTitles
http://bit.ly/ForthcomingKindleTitlesNow

Calibre

$299 for the Kindle 2

$489 for the super-sized Kindle DX

$199.99 for a just-like-new "refurbished" Kindle 1

Manage Your Kindle

Manage Your Kindle Subscriptions

Kindle Nation Daily Blog Website

http://bit.ly/KindleNationArchive

To have Kindle Nation Daily posts pushed directly to your Kindle in real time each day for just 99 cents a month:

http://bit.ly/KindleNationDaily in the Kindle Store

The Kindle Chronicles

Kindle Gift Card

iPhone or iPod Touch

No Kindle Required - The Complete "Kindle for iPhone" User's Guide

m.google.com

http://m.gmail.com

http://www.audible.com/kindle

http://bit.ly/KindlePedia

http://m.facebook.com

http://www.facebook.com/stephen.windwalker

http://m.twitter.com

http://twitter.com/WindwalkerHere

Freebies for Your Kindle

http://bit.ly/FreeKindleStoreBooks

http://bit.ly/FreeKindlePromotionalTitles

http://www.gutenberg.org/wiki/Main_Page

http://freekindlebooks.org/MagicCatalog/MagicCatalog.mobi

http://www.mobileread.com/mobiguide

http://www.feedbooks.com/kindleguide

BooksShouldBeFree.com

http://bit.ly/ForthcomingKindleTitlesNow

http://readingroo.ms/

http://www.fictionwise.com/ebooks/freebooks.htm

http://diesel-ebooks.com/cgi-bin/category/free_download

http://www.readprint.com/

Baen Free Library
Creative Commons
Dartmouth College - Ebooks in the Public Domain
Digital Book Index
Free Techbooks
Google Book Search
Internet Archive
Librivox
MobileRead
Mobipocket
Munseys
Online Books Page
Podiobooks
Project Gutenberg
Technical Books Online
Wikibooks
World Public Library
Wowio

Amazon Store Bestseller Links

Bestsellers in Books
Bestsellers in Magazines
Bestsellers in Amazon Video on Demand
Bestsellers in MP3s and Digital Music (Kindle Compatible)
Bestsellers in Music on Disc

Bestsellers in Computers and Computer Hardware
Bestsellers in Hand-Helds and PDAs
Bestsellers in Office Products
Bestsellers in Software
Bestsellers in Cell Phones and Wireless Service
Bestsellers in Camera, Video, and Photo
Bestsellers in Electronics
Bestsellers in Grocery
Bestsellers in Gourmet Foods
Bestsellers in Home and Personal Care
Bestsellers in Home and Garden
Bestsellers in Jewelry
Bestsellers in Movies and TV on DVD
Bestsellers in Musical Instruments and Musicians' Gear
Bestsellers in Sporting Goods
Bestsellers in Video Games and Consoles
Bestsellers in Toys and Games

Best Blogs
(Top Sellers at Amazon)

Kindle Nation Daily
A Kindle Home Page
A Kindle World
Kindle Store Bestsellers: Blogs Only
Amazon Daily BLOG RSS
Amazon Omnivoracious BLOG RSS
AP Sports Headlines RSS
AP Strange News RSS
AP Top Headlines RSS
Ars Technica RSS
BlogCritics.org Books RSS
Boing Boing RSS
Daily KOS RSS

ESPN Baseball News RSS
ESPN NFL Nation BLOG RSS
ESPN NFL News RSS
Gawker Full Content RSS
Gawker Excerpts RSS
Gawker Top Stories RSS
Gizmodo Full Content RSS
Gizmodo Top Stories Only RSS
Gizmodo Excerpts RSS
Huffington Post BLOG RSS
Knowledge@Wharton RSS
Lifehacker Full Content RSS
Michelle Malkin RSS
MIT Tech Review Top Stories RSS
MIT Tech Review Editor's BLOG RSS
New York Times Breaking News RSS
OhGizmo! RSS
Onion Daily RSS
Overheard in New York RSS
Reuters Business RSS
Reuters Oddly Enough RSS
Reuters Top News RSS
SlashDot RSS
TechCrunch RSS
TV Guide HotList RSS

Blog Lists

BlogCatalog MOBILE / Home RSS
BlogCatalog Directory
BlogCatalog Fiction RSS
BlogFlux Best Blog Sites
BlogLines Most Popular Feeds
BlogLines News RSS

Technorati Top 100 BLOGS
Top 100 Most Subscribed RSS Feeds

Book Catalogs

Amazon: YourMediaLibrary
FaceBook Visual Bookshelf
Fictionwise Bookshelf
LibraryThink MOBILE
ListBook.net
Shelfari MOBILE

Book Reviews

AllReaders
Amazon Daily BLOG RSS
Amazon Omnivoracious BLOG RSS
Asimov's Science Fiction Current Issue
Barnes & Noble MOBILE / RSS Feeds
Barnes & Noble Reviews RSS
Barnes & Noble Spotlight RSS
Barnes & Noble Long List RSS
Barnes & Noble Interview RSS
Billboard Book Reviews RSS
BlogCritics.org Books RSS
BookMarks Magazine
Borders Books
EW.com Books RSS
EW.com Book Reviews RSS
Fantastic Fiction
New York Times Books MOBILE / RSS
New York Times Book Review MOBILE / RSS
New York Times Best Sellers
New York Times First Chapters
Publishers Weekly RSS Feeds

PW Latest News RSS
PW Notes from Bookroom RSS
PW Reviews RSS
Salon Book Reviews RSS
Stop You're Killing Me!
TeleRead RSS
The New Yorker Book Bench RSS
USA Today Book Review RSS
Washington Post Book Review RSS

Business & Finance

AP Business RSS
Bloomberg.com MOBILE
Business Week MOBILE / RSS Feeds
Business Week Most Popular RSS
Business Week Top News RSS
CNNMoney.com RSS
Economist.com / RSS Feeds
Economist Full Print RSS
Forbes MOBILE / RSS Feeds
Forbes Headlines RSS
Forbes Popular Stories RSS
FORTUNE Magazine RSS
FT.com MOBILE
Kiplinger Headlines RSS / RSS Feeds
Knowledge@Wharton RSS
Motley Fool Headlines RSS
New York Times Business RSS
Reuters Business RSS
Schwab MOBILE
Technology News RSS

Comics

Comic Alert RSS List
Comic Book Resources RSS Feeds / RSS
Isnoop's Comic Strip Snagger
Tapestry Comics RSS Directory / RSS

eBook Downloads, Support & Discussions

Amazon MOBILE
Amazon Books MOBILE
Amazon Daily BLOG RSS
Amazon Omnivoracious BLOG RSS
Amazon: Kindle Support
DigitalBookIndex
eBook Reporter RSS
eBooks.com
eBooks.com Featured Titles RSS
eLibrary.net
eReader.com
FeedBooks MOBILE / GUIDE
FeedBooks BLOG RSS
FeedBooks Most Recent Books RSS
FeedBooks Most Downloaded RSS
Free-ebooks.net
Free ebooks AU
Free Books for Your Kindle
ManyBooks.net MOBILE
ManyBooks.net New Titles RSS
Project Gutenberg
The Online Books Page
WIT Guides.com
World Public Library Association

Entertainment

ABC MOBILE
AOL MovieFone MOBILE / WAP
AOL MovieFone New in Theaters RSS
AOL MovieFone New on DVD RSS
AOL MovieFone Top Movie News RSS
AP Entertainment RSS
AP Strange News RSS
Astrology & Horoscopes
Billboard MOBILE / RSS Feeds
Billboard News RSS
CBS MOBILE
Discovery Channel MOBILE / RSS
E! Entertainment MOBILE / RSS
Fandango MOBILE
FOX News Entertainment RSS
Flickr MOBILE
Gawker Full Content RSS
Gawker Excerpts RSS
Gawker Top Stories RSS
History Channel MOBILE
Hollywood.com Entertainment RSS
MSN Entertainment RSS
MSN Entertainment MOBILE / RSS Feeds
MSN Entertainment Just-In News RSS
MTV Latest News RSS / RSS Feeds
NBC MOBILE
NetFlix MOBILE
Overheard in New York RSS
People Magazine Latest News RSS
People Magazine Celeb Photos RSS
People Magazine StyleWatch News RSS
PVR Blog RSS

Readers Digest What's New RSS
Readers Digest Advice RSS
Readers Digest Living Healthy RSS
Readers Digest Your America RSS
Reuters Entertainment RSS
Salon Entertainment RSS
ShowBIZ Data MOBILE
Star Magazine RSS
The Internet Movie Database (IMDb)
TicketMaster
TLC MOBILE / Highlights RSS
TV Guide MOBILE / HotList RSS
WBZ Entertainment RSS
Variety Headlines RSS
Yahoo Entertainment MOBILE

Hobbies

American Crossword Puzzle Tournament
CRUCIVERB.com
Crossword Blogs RH
Crossword News RH

Kindle Blogs

Kindle Nation Daily
A Kindle Home Page
A Kindle World
Amazon's Kindle Blog / RSS
BlogKindle RSS
eBook Reporter RSS / Comments
ebookVINE RSS
indieKindle RSS / Comments
Kindle Buzz RSS

Kindle Chat RSS / Comments
Kindle Chronicles RSS
KindleKorner Yahoo Group
KindleOwner RSS / Comments
Kindle Pages RSS
KindleReader RSS
KindleVille RSS
MobileRead Forums RSS
Print is Dead RSS
Technorati List of Kindle BLOGS
TeleRead RSS
The Book of Kindle RSS
WorldPress Kindle Guide RSS / Comments

Kindle Gear

The Kindle DX
The Kindle 2
The Kindle 1
Kindle Accessories
Kindle Store Bestsellers
Amazon.com MOBILE
Amazon Kindle Store
Amazon Kindle Books
Bigger & Brighter
iGo Power Adapters
LightWedge
M-Edge Covers
Mighty Bright Lights
Oberon Design Covers
VanMobile Gear
WaterField Cases

Magazines

Kindle Store Bestsellers: Magazines & Journals Only
Discover Magazine RSS
Harpers Magazine
Salon MOBILE / RSS Feeds
Salon Main RSS
Slate Magazine MOBILE / RSS
The New Yorker / RSS Feeds BLOGS
The New Yorker Book Bench RSS

Mail & Message

AOL / MOBILE
Facebook MOBILE
Gmail MOBILE
MSM Hotmail MOBILE
MySpace MOBILE
VerizonCentral
VerizonWebMail
YahooMail MOBILE / MOBILE Beta

Mobile RSS Readers

Alesti RSS Reader
BlogLinesMobile NewBeta FullSite
DailyLit
FeedBucket
FeedOnFeeds
FeedShow
GoogleReader / MOBILE
LiteFeeds
My Yahoo MOBILE / DESKTOP

RocketReader
RSS Daily News / S
RSS-Feed Reader
Web Feed Reader

Mobile Transcoders

BareSite
EchoDitto Full-Text RSS
Google Reader
Google Reader MOBILE / Transcoder
Mowser
Phonifier
Skweezer Enter URL / BMK DIR SET BLOG

Mobile Site Lists

PDA Hotspots MOBILE
PdaWebSites.com MOBILE
Pocket PC Magazine MOBILE
Cantoni.mobi MOBILE
My Mobile Experience MOBILE
PDAportal.com MOBILE
Skweezer Directory
Web On Your Cell MOBILE

Newspapers

**(Downloaded from Feedbooks to your
Kindle Home Screen and read offline)**

Amazon Feeds {ac} MOBI
Aruba Feeds {ac} MOBI

Boston Globe {ac} MOBI
Ebook Feeds {ac} MOBI
Kindle Feeds {ac} MOBI
Littleton Independent {ac} MOBI
News Feeds {ac} MOBI
Reference Feeds {ac} MOBI
Salon Magazine {ac} MOBI
Tech Feeds {ac} MOBI
Business Week MOBI
Economist MOBI
Economist Full Print Edition MOBI
Engadget MOBI
Gadget Newspaper MOBI
iLiad eBook Newspaper MOBI
Kindle & Ebook News MOBI
Kindleville MOBI
New York Times MOBI
New York Times Books MOBI
New Yorker MOBI
Newsweek MOBI
Reuters MOBI
Tech News MOBI
Time Magazine MOBI
USA Today MOBI
Wall Street Journal MOBI
Washington Post MOBI
Wired Top Stories MOBI

News: National

ABC News MOBILE / RSS Feeds
ABC News Top Stories RSS
AP Home / RSS Feeds
AP Top Headlines RSS

Atlantic / Current-RSS
BBC News Online MOBILE / RSS Feeds
Canada.com MOBILE / RSS Feeds
CBC Top Stories RSS
CBS News MOBILE / RSS Feeds
CBS News Top Stories RSS
CNN MOBILE / RSS Feeds
CNN Top Stories RSS
CNN Recent Stories RSS
CNN US RSS
CNN World RSS
Daily KOS RSS
FOX News MOBILE / RSS Feeds
FOX News Latest Headlines RSS
Google News MOBILE / RSS
Huffington Post MOBILE / RSS Feeds
Huffington Post Full Feed RSS
Huffington Post Latest News RSS
Huffington Post BLOG RSS
Huffington Post Featured Posts RSS
LA Daily News / MOBILE RSS Feeds
LA Times MOBILE / RSS Feeds
Michelle Malkin RSS
MSN MOBILE / RSS Feeds
MSNBC MOBILE / RSS Feeds
MSNBC Top Headlines RSS
MSNBC US News RSS
MSNBC World News RSS
MSNBC Hot in Health RSS
NASA News RSS / RSS Feeds
National Geographic News RSS
New York Times MOBILE / RSS Feeds
New York Times Home Page RSS
NEWS.com MOBILE

Newsweek MOBILE / RSS Feeds
Newsweek Top Stories RSS
Onion MOBILE / Onion Daily RSS
Reuters MOBILE / RSS Feeds
Reuters Oddly Enough RSS
Reuters Top News RSS
Reuters US News RSS
Salon News & Politics RSS
TIME MOBILE / RSS Feeds
Time Top Stories RSS
US News & World Report MOBILE / MINI
US News & World Report RSS Feeds
US News & World Report Home RSS
USA Today MOBILE / RSS Feeds
USA Today Top Headlines RSS
Wall Street Journal MOBILE / RSS Feeds
Wall Street Journal US News RSS
Washington Post MOBILE / RSS Feeds
Washington Post Top News RSS
World News / Classic
World News International News RSS
Yahoo News MOBILE / RSS Feeds
Yahoo News Top Stories RSS

News: Sports

AP Sports RSS
APA RSS
AzBilliards News Feed RSS
BBC SPORT
Billiards Digest / Calendar
CNN Sports RSS
CueSportTV / Calendar
CyclingNews.com

Daily Racing Form
ESPN MOBILE / RSS Feeds
ESPN Top Headlines RSS
ESPN Baseball News RSS ESPN NFL Nation BLOG RSS
ESPN NFL News RSS
ESPN NHL News RSS
ESPN Poker News RSS
FOX Sports RSS
GG.COM Horse Racing
GOLF.com RSS
Golf Digest
MLB Scores MOBILE
NASCAR MOBILE
NBA MOBILE
New York Times Sports RSS
NFL MOBILE / Headlines RSS
Onion Sports RSS
Ozone Billiards / Calendar
Poolmag's 8-Ball BLOG RSS
Sports Illustrated MOBILE
Sports Illustrated Top Stories RSS
Sports Illustrated Latest Stories RSS
SportsLine MOBILE / RSS Feeds
SportsLine Top Stories RSS
The Sporting News MOBILE
TSN Canada RSS
USA Today Sports RSS
World Wrestling Entertainment MOBILE / RSS Feeds
WPBA.com / Calendar
Yahoo Sports MOBILE
Yahoo Sports Top News RSS

News: Technology

AP Technology RSS
Boing Boing MOBILE / RSS
Business Week Technology Reviews RSS
CNET MOBILE / RSS Feeds
CNET Latest News MOBILE / RSS Feeds
CNET Tech News MOBILE
CNET Gadget News RSS
CNET Editors Choice Reviews RSS
CNET Most Recent Reviews RSS
CNET News Main Feed RSS
ComputerWorld News RSS
Engadget MOBILE / RSS
eWeek Technology News RSS
GadgetReview RSS
Gadget Reviews RSS
Gadget Reviews.org RSS
Gizmodo Full Content RSS
Gizmodo Top Stories Only RSS
Gizmodo Excerpts RSS
Gravitational Pull RSS / Comments
InformationWeek RSS / RSS Feeds
InfoWorld Top Headlines RSS
MIT Tech Review Top Stories RSS
MIT Tech Review Editor's BLOG RSS
MIT Tech Review RSS Feeds
Mobile Magazine Online RSS
MSNBC Tech & Gadgets RSS
New York Times Bits BLOG RSS
OhGizmo! RSS
PCMagazine MOBILE / RSS Feeds
PCMagazine News MOBILE
PCMagazine Reviews MOBILE
PCMagazine Breaking News RSS
PCMagazine New Product Reviews RSS

Reuters Technology RSS
Scientific American News RSS / RSS Feeds
Slashdot MOBILE / RSS
TechCrunch RSS
TechDirt RSS
TechNet Magazine RSS
The Gadgeteer MOBILE / RSS
The Raw Feed RSS
Wired MOBILE / RSS Feeds
Wired Top Stories RSS
Wired Gadgets RSS
Wired Software RSS
Wired Gadget Lab BLOG
ZDNet MOBILE / RSS Feeds
ZDNet Blogs RSS
ZDNet Product Reviews RSS
ZDNet Tech News RSS
ZDNet Mobile Gadgeteer MOBILE / RSS BLOG

Reference

4INFO MOBILE
Answers.com MOBILE
Bibliomania
Birding News RSS
Dictionary.com MOBILE
Dictionary.com Word of the Day RSS
GasBuddy MOBILE
Google MOBILE / Mobile Products
Google Directions MOBILE
How Stuff Works
MapQuest MOBILE
Motorcycle Events MOBILE
MSN Quote of the Day RSS
MSN This day in History RSS

MSN Words of the Day RSS
My Yahoo MOBILE
National Weather Service MOBILE
Orbitz MOBILE
Restaurant Row MOBILE
Song Lyrics MOBILE
Today in History (Boston.com) RSS
Traffic MOBILE
USA.gov MOBILE
ViewTraffic.net Live Traffic
WhitePages MOBILE / Company BLOG RSS
Wikipedia MOBILE / Recent Changes RSS
Yahoo Map MOBILE
YellowPages / MOBILE
Yelp MOBILE
Zondervan Bible Search MOBILE

Shipping Carriers

UPS MOBILE
USPS

Shopping

Amazon.com
BestBuy MOBILE
ebay MOBILE
Half.com
HomeDepot / MOBILE
JCPenny
PriceGrabber MOBILE
SalesCircular.com
Shopzilla
Walmart

Travel

AA Domestic Next Weekend Net SAAver Fares RSS
AAA MOBILE
American Airlines MOBILE
Amtrak MOBILE
Aruba News RSS
Aruba News (FeedZilla) RSS
Aruba News (Topix) RSS
Aruba News at NYTimes RSS
Aruba Tax & Financial News
Aruba Today
Aruba Travel News RSS
VistAruba.com
Boston Coach MOBILE
CheapTickets / RSS Feeds
Continental Airlines MOBILE
Delta Air Lines MOBILE
Exxon/Mobile Locator MOBILE
FastLane Account
HRS Hotel Reservation Service MOBILE
JetBlue MOBILE
Last Minute Deals
Northwest Airlines MOBILE
Orbitz MOBILE
Southwest Airlines MOBILE
Travelocity.com MOBILE
United Airlines MOBILE
US Airways MOBILE

Weather

AccuWeather.com
Bureau of Meteorology
Foreca MOBILE
Get My Weather.net
National Weather Service MOBILE
The Weather Network (Canada)
Weather Channel National RSS
Weather Channel BLOG RSS
Weather.com MOBILE
Weather Underground MOBILE
Yahoo Weather MOBILE

Glossary

"MOBILE" is a link for a site that is already formatted for mobile devices.

"RSS" is an RSS feed that has been reformatted for mobile devices, usually by Skweezer or Google.

Part Two:
What's New with the Kindle 2

Fifteen months after Amazon launched its first Kindle, the Kindle 2 arrived on the scene in February 2009 with a price of $359, which was reduced to $299 about three months later.

Amazon ramped up production capacity to try to avoid the shipping backlogs that sometimes frustrated Kindle 1 buyers, and shipments have been going out to Amazon customers since February 23, 2009 without any delays.

"Kindle 2 is everything customers tell us they love about the original Kindle, only thinner, faster, crisper, with longer battery life, and capable of holding hundreds more books. If you want, Kindle 2 will even read to you — something new we added that a book could never do," said Amazon.com founder and CEO Jeff Bezos at the Kindle 2 "launch" press conference February 9, 2009 at New York's Morgan Museum and Library.

"While we're excited about Kindle 2, we know that great hardware is useless without vast selection. That's why the Kindle Store offers customers over 230,000 books."

That 230,000-book figure – long since outdated, since the figure is now pushing 350,000 as of late Summer 2009 – may be the least impressive aspect of Amazon's progress with the Kindle so far, if only because Bezos has set the bar so high in his repeated references to an objective of making "every book ever published" available on the Kindle. After all, given the fact that at least 200,000 new book titles are added each year now in the U.S. alone, it would be fair to conclude that the Kindle catalog has actually lost ground as it has grown from under 90,000 titles at the time of the Kindle 1 launch in November 2007 to the present 350,000-title figure.

However, perhaps 2008 was the year for Amazon to blaze the Kindle trail, and 2009 and 2010 will be the years for publishers to populate it. Let's focus here, first, on some dramatic new developments, and some other features that happily stayed the same, with the Kindle 2.

I. A Sleek New Hardware Package

From an Ugly Duckling to a Swan

While it's certainly true that most of the people who own a first-generation Kindle are steadfast in their love for it, few of them would try to make the claim that the device is beautiful, sleek, or elegant. With the totally new, slimmed-down design of the Kindle 2, all that has changed. Although at 8 inches by 5.3 inches it has about four times the palmprint of the iPhone or the iPod Touch, the new Kindle model has the sleek feel and look that we might associate with an Apple product, and at only 0.36 inches is only half as thick as the old Kindle. The placement of the page-turning buttons is much more self-contained, so that the old Kindle 1 users' bane of gratuitous page-turning is now a non-issue. You will be able to handle and hold the Kindle in whatever way best suits your reading mode without fear that you are issuing unintended commands.

No SD Card Slot, but Seven Times
The Storage Capacity of the Kindle 1

"You can fit *how many books* on that little thing?"

That's right, 1500.

The original Kindle came with about 200 megabytes of storage, with a slot for secondary storage on an SD memory card.

You can save the money that you might have spent for an SD card for the Kindle 2. There's no slot for the card, and there doesn't need to be, because the native memory storage onboard the Kindle 2 is two gigabytes, of which about 1.4 gigabytes is available for your content. That's enough for 1500 books.

Keep in mind that non-text content such as pictures, music, podcasts and audiobooks ties up a lot more storage capacity than text, so if you migrate your entire MP3 collection and all your Facebook photographs to the Kindle 2, well, you won't get anywhere near 1500 books.

As with the Kindle 1, you can count on Amazon to create automatic backup files of every book you purchase from the Kindle Store. It is now easier than ever, even after you have deleted titles from your Kindle, to access and re-download them from Amazon without any new or additional cost. A list of these titles is available directly from the Kindle Home Screen when you select "Archived items." Just use the 5-way to select a title from the list, with your Kindle's wireless Whispernet on, to download the title within seconds.

One previously available feature that Amazon has abandoned, unfortunately, involves Kindle owners' option of refreshing the content of books they have purchased from the Kindle Store easily at any time in order to receive newly available content updates. This feature was available when the Kindle was first introduced, but apparently it came into conflict with other technical imperatives.

The Crisper, Faster Kindle 2 Display

The Kindle 2's E-Ink electronic paper display still specs out with a 6-inch diagonal size and 600 x 800 pixel resolution at 167 ppi, but it's a big improvement over its predecessor in two important ways: crispness and refresh speed.

Many Kindle 1 owners were mildly annoyed at the split-second flash that occurs each time a "page" is turned on the original model. The Kindle 2 refresh rate is, on average, 20 per cent faster than the first-generation unit.

Equally important is the enhanced screen crispness that comes with upgrading the display from 4 grayscale shades to the Kindle 2's 16 shades. This feature results in text that is crisper and easier on the eyes, and allows a vast improvement in the look and accessibility of onscreen graphics including charts and tables, pictures or covers in the books and periodicals that you're reading, and photographs you upload to your Kindle.

The overall effect remains consistent with one of the big selling points of the original Kindle as a reading device: the gadget disappears into the book you are reading because it has the appearance of real ink on paper, with no backlighting, no glare or eyestrain, and no problem if you want to read in the sunshine on the beach, the hammock, or the back porch. As with the previous version, the Kindle 2 display only draws power from the battery when turning a page.

Enhanced Design and Placement of Buttons, Switches, Bars and Keyboard

While the slimmer, sleeker Kindle 2 package is drawing plenty of kudos from those who believe in the importance of elegant tech design, an equally significant transformation comes at the meeting place of form and function, where the Kindle 2 is vastly improved.

The previous- and next-page buttons that ran almost the entire length of the Kindle 1, and made gratuitous page-turning so annoying, are gone. They are replaced by appropriately sized buttons on either side of the Kindle, along with a Home button placed appropriately just above the right-hand next-page button.

Just below that right-hand next-page button is the real input center of the Kindle 2, the 5-way joystick-like controller that allows Kindle users to make the most of the Kindle 2's much more highly realized screen navigation features. This "5-way," as we'll call it here, is grouped nicely with the Kindle 2 Menu button and Back button. (See the next section for more detail on the 5-way.)

One result of these design improvements is that you seldom need to use the Kindle's tiny keyboard unless you are actually typing something on the Kindle screen for purposes such as annotation, search, URL entry, or email inputting. Many Kindle users will go weeks on end without having to exercise their thumbs on the keyboard. However, it is well worth typing in a word or phrase to help you get accustomed to the powerful search features of the Kindle. The traditional bibliographic convention of a book index is a gratuitous duplication in many Kindle editions. It is so much easier, faster, and more comprehensive to type in a word or two and let the Kindle complete a global search of the document and render clickable results on its display almost instantaneously.

Chances are good that within a day or two you'll be comfortable enough with the 5-way to make it your primary navigational tool. But don't overlook the "Back" button. Many users never touch it because they assume that it duplicates the "Previous Page" button's function, but in fact it provides a handy way to retrace your steps on the Kindle. The previous-page and next-page buttons, of course, take you through any document you are reading on your Kindle a page at a time.

The Kindle 2 also does far better with the placement of the power switch, the wireless On-Off switch, the headphone jack and the volume control than its predecessor. On Kindle 1, you had to remove the Kindle from its cover to access the power and wireless switches on the back of the unit; now the power switch is on the top edge and the wireless switch is on the display screen itself, as a toggle command at the top of any menu screen that displays when you press the Menu button from anywhere on your Kindle 2. You'll find the headphone jack just to the right of the power switch on the top edge, and the volume controls at the top of the right edge. As with the Kindle 1, the USB/Power port and the battery charge indicator light are together on the bottom edge of the Kindle 2.

A 5-Way Joystick Controller
For Better OnScreen Navigation

Amazon has also greatly improved the processes of note-taking and highlighting text by replacing the old Kindle scrollwheel and the somewhat bizarre right-margin silvery cursor. In their place is a joystick-like 5-way controller that allows precise movement of an onscreen cursor both horizontally and vertically on the Kindle 2 display. This precision also makes it possible to move or "jump" between sections and articles as you are reading a newspaper, magazine or blog, which is a great improvement over the clunky old process of moving through the morning paper (or any other periodical) one maddeningly slow screen refresh at a time. For the sake of simplicity and sentence flow, and without intending any reference to TV programs such as *Swingtown* or *Big Love*, I'll refer to this 5-way joystick-like controller throughout this book as the "5-way."

To state what will be obvious to you as soon as you have used the 5-way, the 5th "way" -- after up, down, left and right -- refers to the fact that pressing down on the 5-way is just like clicking with a mouse, trackball or trackpad: it selects the item on which you are clicking for whatever process is appropriate, such as following an internal or external link or selecting an option from a menu, or you can use it to look up a word in your Kindle dictionary. Use the 5-way to place the cursor next to any single word and a definition will show up instantly on your screen.

You can also use the 5-way to capture and look up a longer phrase without the need to type it into your Kindle's search field. Just click to the left of the first word in the phrase, move the cursor as far along as you wish, and without clicking again press "Menu" and select "Search This Book." The entire phrase will appear in the search field and you can then move the 5-way to the right to select "Find [in the same book]," "my items," "store," "google," "Wikipedia" or "dictionary."

Finally, you can use the 5-way to navigate among a sensible and intuitive set of Kindle 2 menus instead of having to schlep through a Kindle 1 navigation process of slow, step-at-a-time backward and forward movements that frequently froze your screen just as you were about to say a hopeful "Eureka."

Dual Rear-Mounted Stereo Speakers
For Improved Hands-Free Listening

Confession: I never complained about the tinny mono speaker on the Kindle 1 because I didn't want to be the only one complaining, or the only one admitting that I don't particularly like wearing headphones, earbuds, or anything else but a hat on my head. Besides, what was there to listen to on the Kindle 1? You could load a podcast or a few songs of what Amazon called "background music," but you'd quickly tie up a large portion of the Kindle 1's native storage memory.

But now that the Kindle 2 offers a text-to-voice "Read to Me" feature, a lot more of us will want to listen to the device itself, hands-free, while we are doing other things that might make wires, headsets and earbuds inconvenient or unsafe. So I'm pleased with myself for having had the courage to speak up and persuade Amazon to upgrade its "sound system" to a much easier-on-the-ears set of rear-mounted stereo speakers. Okay, you already know I played no role in this decision.

But now, with the presence of improved audio and the 10-fold increase in native storage capacity from Kindle 1 to Kindle 2, it may actually make sense to transfer some podcasts or set up a little playlist.

Addition by Subtraction: Designer Covers for the Kindle 2

A few weeks before the press conference to launch the Kindle 2, I posted information on my website to the effect that the Kindle 2 price would be about 10 per cent higher than the Kindle 1. I was wrong, except in the sense that I was right.

What Amazon did, instead of raising the price for the Kindle 2, was to detach the Kindle cover from the Kindle unit purchase. The original Kindle 1 cover from Amazon was a fairly cheap-looking faux leather item that was included in the box with the Kindle for the $359 purchase price and did not come close enough to the Moleskine appearance that Amazon was perhaps hoping for to keep tens (perhaps hundreds) of thousands of Kindle owners from buying third-party covers from M-Edge, Kroo, Octovo and others.

With the Kindle 2, Amazon no longer bundles in the Kindle's "book cover," but sells a more elegant Amazon-manufactured genuine black leather cover, with soft suede interior, for $29.99. Amazon says that the cover's "integrated attachment hinge" ensures a secure fit – something that was not available with the Kindle 1 cover without a fair amount of creative intervention – and has gone so far as to apply for a patent for the hinge. The fact that the Kindle 2 has a sleek, symmetrical shape makes it much easier to outfit and accessorize elegantly than the wedge-shaped Kindle 1, and during the first week after the launch of the Kindle 2 it seemed clear that Amazon's decision to monetize the cover separately was working out just fine. The Kindle 2 cover, which weighs almost as much as the Kindle 2 itself, took an early lead as the top-selling Kindle 2 accessory in the Kindle Store, just ahead of a pricey $65 two-year extended warranty offered by Amazon subsidiary Service Net Solutions.

Meanwhile, the fact that the Kindle cover is not automatically included in the box will be a boon to third-party manufacturers and sellers of alternative covers for the Kindle. The Kindle Store has rolled out an impressive array of designer covers from Patagonia, Cole-Haan, and Belkin as well as some stylish new covers from M-Edge that can be transformed into attractive hands-free reading platforms. Prices range from $24.99 all the way up to over a hundred dollars, but at least you won't feel like you are spending money to replace a standard, in-the-box cover that has already been shipped to you.

The New Kindle Battery and Charging Options

The Kindle 2 comes with a more powerful, non-replaceable battery that, according to Amazon's claims, should provide 25 per cent longer life between charges. Amazon's claim is that the Kindle 2 will hold a full charge for two weeks of reading with the wireless turned off, or four to five days of reading with the wireless turned on. These standards, if true, will amount to far more than a 25 per cent improvement in the experience of many Kindle 1 owners. Use of Kindle 2 audio features such as "Read-to-Me" will discharge the battery more rapidly than simple use of the display for reading with the wireless feature turned off.

The Kindle 2's power charger has been redesigned for greater portability, but many owners of the new Kindle will be even more pleased to learn that they can now recharge their Kindle batteries even more simply by plugging the device's USB cable into their computer. The USB-based battery recharging process can be especially helpful if you're traveling. Older USB connections or secondary USB connections (such as one might find on a computer's keyboard) may not be effective in fully recharging your Kindle 2.

Of course, since the USB cable connection with a computer ordinarily disables the Kindle as a reading device while the connection is active, the Kindle 2 also comes with a faster-charging universal power adapter that is designed to work worldwide. To use this power adapter outside the United States, it's necessary to plug it into a physical plug adapter that's been approved for the country in which you're located. (Note: If you wish to use your Kindle for reading or other purposes while it's connected to your computer for charging, just go into the "Finder" or "My Computer" window on your computer and click on "Eject." In most instances the Kindle 2 will continue to draw a charge from your computer, but will be available for reading and other normal uses).

Some current and prospective Kindle owners have expressed concern that the fact that the Kindle 2's battery is not user-replaceable may indicate the likelihood of planned obsolescence for the Kindle 2. Although I don't share this worry, I do think that it indicates the likelihood of a more expensive planned battery-replacement cost than was necessary with the Kindle 1, whose user-replaceable replacement battery sells for $19.95 on those occasions when it's actually in stock. The understanding I've gleaned from Amazon is that Amazon will replace the Kindle 2 battery free of charge if it ceases to function while your Kindle 2 is under its free one-year warranty. After the warranty expires, I'm told that Amazon will charge $59 to replace a Kindle 2 battery.

The additional problem, of course, is that either of these procedures would presumably require a Kindle owner to send her

Kindle in for the procedure and thus be without her beloved Kindle for days, which is a terrible thing to have to endure. My hope is that Amazon will instead seek to emulate Apple's seamless customer service in such matters: on the two occasions when one of my family's iPods has required some repair or other intervention, Apple customer service has overnighted me a new iPod to keep, along with a package for my prompt return of its functionally challenged predecessor.

One positive consequence that I anticipate with the fixed, inaccessible battery in the Kindle 2 is fewer freeze-ups than I experienced with the original Kindle. I never went anywhere with my Kindle 1 without a pushpin or paper clip for use in the reset pinhole. The Kindle 2 can accommodate a cold reset without the use of any foreign objects: just disconnect the device (from both a power outlet and a USB connection), then slide and hold the power switch for 15 seconds before you release it.

If your new Kindle is just the latest in what is starting to seem like an endless wave of devices that require USB connectivity with your computer, perhaps it is time to bring some organization to your USB connections. The CyberPower High-Speed 7-Port USB Hub comes highly recommended by Amazon reviewers, ships free with Amazon Prime, fits in the palm of your hand, and retails for less than $30.

What's Inside the Kindle 2

Like the Kindle 1, the Kindle 2 is a mobile computer built on the Linux platform, which allows its creators at Amazon's Lab 126 in Cupertino to provide an impressive, targeted range of specific features in a stripped-down, technologically economical package. About 600 MB of the Kindle's 2 GB of flash memory are dedicated to the software and systems that manage the device, leaving approximately 1.4 GB for your Kindle-compatible content.

The Kindle 2 display is patented by Cambridge, Massachusetts company e-Ink and manufactured in Taiwan. It has been upgraded to 16 grayscale shades from the four shades available on the Kindle 1. The display technology involves million of microcapsules that act as pixels in order to provide a sharp but easy-on-the-eyes black, white and gray display on the Kindle's 600x800-pixel screen. These microcapsules are driven by a layer of transparent electrodes that consume power only when refreshing or turning a page and are far more energy-efficient than LCD displays. The refresh speed of the Kindle 2 display is about 20 per cent faster than the Kindle 1.

Thanks to a great job by the folks at ifixit.com, we can tell you the following about the generally impressive innards of the Kindle 2:

* The Kindle 2's more powerful non-replaceable battery is a 3.7 V lithium polymer battery that weights just over 30 grams, about one-tenth of the total Kindle 2 weight. Battery power management is handled by a Freescale MC13783VK5 chip.

* The Kindle 2 logic board includes a variety of chips manufactured by Freescale, Samsung, Epson and others.

* The primary Kindle 2 "brain" or processor chip is a fast 532 MHz, ARM-11 90nm 14mm package from Freescale.

* To its right are two SDRAM chips manufactured by Samsung, including a 32MB mobile DDR chip.

* The Kindle 2 flash memory and controller reside in the large 2 GB moviNAND package introduced by Samsung in 2006 and used in many mobile devices.

II. An Enhanced, More User-Friendly Kindle Reading Environment

Let Your Kindle Read to You
With a New "Read-to-Me" Feature

Among the more intriguing innovations in the Kindle 2 is a "Text-to-Speech" Read-to-Me feature wherein a somewhat creepy and robotic "voice" will read aloud to you from any text file that you purchase or otherwise acquire and download to the device. Whether it's the latest *New Yorker*, a memo your boss sent you, or *The Brothers Karamazov*, the Kindle 2 will read it aloud while you are cooking, driving, or dozing off (hopefully not in that order), turn its own pages for you, and mark your place in case you wish to return to more active reading later. Once you open any text document on your Kindle – including books, magazines, newspapers, blogs, and your own documents – you can choose either to read it on the display screen or to have the Kindle read the document aloud to you in either a male or female voice. You can easily toggle back and forth between spoken word and onscreen reading, and the Kindle 2 will keep your place, turn the pages for you as you listen, and adjust its spoken-word reading speed to suit your preferences. I fully expect that a future volume of DSM-IV will have a name for at least one syndrome originating from its victims' childhood experience of having been forced to listen to bedtime stories read by the Kindle 2. Personally, although I rarely use the feature with more literary texts, I actually prefer it with certain kinds of news material in periodical, blog, or article form.

Read-to-Me is easy to find and activate with the 5-way on your Kindle. Somewhat appropriately, it's on the same pop-up screen as the Kindle's adjustable font options. Just press the "text" key (**Aa**) on the bottom row of the keyboard, just to the right of the spacebar. In addition to your choice of six adjustable font sizes, you'll also see "Text-to-Speech" with an on-off toggle switch to the right, and choices below to allow you to regulate both the rate of speech and the gender of the monotoned speaking voice. The volume control, as you'll recall, is near the top of the right edge of the Kindle 2.

You should find it easy to switch back and forth between listening and active reading. You can also pause the "Text-to-Speech" feature at any time simply by pressing the spacebar. The Kindle will do the work of turning pages and holding your place while it's reading to you. "Text-to-Speech" is not limited to books that you buy in the Kindle Store. Except for those titles -- mainly from Random House and its many imprints and subsidiaries -- for which Text-to-Speech has been disabled, it will work with any document that you can read on your Kindle including newspapers, magazines, blogs, personal documents, and public domain books and files that you acquire from sources other than the Kindle Store. For most Kindle titles, the Kindle Store product display page informs you, prior to purchase, whether or not Text-to-Speech is enabled.

However creepy or psychologically scarring it may be under some circumstances, Read-to-Me scores high enough on the convenient and cool gadgetry scales that Amazon may have a clear winner: a feature that will drive Kindle device and book sales by adding new and special value to the books and other content that people buy from the Kindle Store. Amazon and its Kindle already have a huge edge on ebook competitors based on access to publishers, front- and mid-list titles, and readers and their credit card information and practices. Read-to-Me will only magnify that edge, if it survives.

Amazon has labeled the read-to-me feature "experimental," which means that it reserves the right to discontinue it at any time. When the Kindle 1 came out, one of its "experimental" features was the Whispernet wireless web, which was a great selling point and a keeper of an idea. But another "experimental" feature was an idea so goofy that, well, it must have come right from the top, in order to make it as far as the Kindle 1 launch. It was called "NowNow" – think Ask Jeeves meets the Kindle, but just don't ask Jeeves any questions about Amazon *or* the Kindle! – and it was neither a keeper nor even a starter.

So, why is Amazon applying the experimental label to its "Text-to-Speech" innovation?

Those of us inclined to put two and two together may divine some connection between the "experimental" hedge and the fact that Author's Guild executive director Paul Aiken has come out swinging against "Text-to-Speech" with the distinct sound of a man who is speaking to copyright attorneys about an authors' rights lawsuit.

"We're studying this matter closely and will report back to you," says the Author's Guild website, and it advises authors to be tenacious with their ebook rights. The website also notes that audiobooks "surpassed $1 billion in sales in 2007," much higher than ebook sales. After all, principles can be much more compelling when they are backed up by 10-figure revenues.

The Author's Guild is not widely known as a particularly democratic, open, or truly author-driven organization – compared, say, with PEN or the National Writer's Union – but it has received plenty of ink lately with a reasonably successful legal settlement against Google Book Search and a less effective campaign against the Amazon Marketplace used book portal. At times the Guild has diminished its own gravitas by taking positions such as one which was widely interpreted to question the right of libraries to lend books to their patrons.

Amazon's attorneys are no slouches, and most of the smart money and the smart people are on Amazon's side here. When lawyers parse these issues they may make distinctions between public and private practices and between recordings and the transitory rendering of a purchased text in audio form.

If Paul Aiken should walk into a public performance hall at some point and find a Kindle propped up at a lectern reading aloud to a crowd of rapt listeners, he should by all means make a citizen's arrest. But a copyright case targeting Kindle customers who purchase an electronic book file and then use available software to listen to part or all of it in the privacy of their homes seems as laughable as the one about the library books.

Still and all, as much as I am hoping to enjoying listening to my Kindle 2 read to me, discreetly, for years to come, I wonder if this "Text-to-Speech" kerfuffle may lead us into a further roiling of the waters. After all, this "Text-to-Speech" software is the product of Nuance, the Massachusetts software developer behind the popular Dragon Speaking Naturally "Speech-to-Text" programs. To my knowledge, nobody yet has sufficiently hacked Amazon's DRM-laden .AZW Kindle text files to open them up beyond the Kindle Store where untold acts of piracy might be lurking, but if "Text-to-Speech" starts talking to "Speech-to-Text," all bets are off.

Late in February 2009, Amazon announced that it would allow "rightsholders," i.e., the authors or publishers who hold the copyright for works available in the Kindle Store, the opportunity to decide on a case-by-case basis whether to make their works accessible with the Kindle 2's "Read-to-Me" feature. Stay tuned, but my expectation is that most authors and publishers will choose to participate in the text-to-speech program, since it adds value to their work in the eyes of many Kindle owners and could therefore be expected to enhance their sales. Six months after Amazon's compromise, most publishers – with the notable exception of Random House and its many imprints – were still sticking with "Read-to-Me."

Hands-Free Reading Options

There are three things you should consider if you want to use the Kindle 2 for hands-free reading:

* First, you already know about this one because I have fallen all over myself gushing over it – the Kindle 2's nifty "Text-to-Speech" Read-to-Me feature. One important Read-to-Me feature that may greatly enhance your ability to follow along as the Kindle reads aloud to you, is your ability to pause the reading (or restart it) by tapping the Kindle's spacebar one time.

* Second, go to the Kindle 2 accessories page and check out the new M-Edge Platform Jackets for the Kindle 2, which

stand up elegantly for hands-free Kindle reading and can also accommodate a book light. Although the more style-conscious among us may be willing to dish out $44.99 for the genuine leather covers in several colors, I couldn't help but notice that the faux leather M-Edge Platform Jackets are very handsome at the exact same $29.99 price point that one would have to pay for Amazon's branded, standard Kindle cover.

* Third, if you are somebody who thinks of reading as a hands-on enterprise, and can't think of any reason why you would want to use your Kindle on a hands-free basis, well, here's one: there are some great cookbooks now available for the Kindle, including a major new Kindle exclusive cookbook from Cook's Illustrated that, at this writing, is being offered free of charge to Kindle owners. Of course, if you're going to cook with the Kindle, you'll want to pick up one of those nifty hands-free platform covers from M-Edge that I mentioned above.

Oh, and one last thing to consider about hands-free reading with the Kindle 2. The only one of these that will work when you are driving an automobile is the "Text-to-Speech" Read-to-Me feature. Trying to read from the display screen while you are driving is a pretty effective way of ensuring that you will read a lot fewer books during the remainder of your life than you might hope.

Improved Navigation of Periodicals

As convenient as it may have been to have the New York Times or any dozens of other newspapers pushed to our Kindles before we rise each morning, internal navigation was challenging and certainly never became as second nature as flipping through the newsprint pages or even reading on a computer. The navigation process is significantly more seamless on the Kindle 2. Just move the 5-way to the left or right to go to the previous or next article in a section, then push down the 5-way to display the complete section list for any newspaper, magazine, or properly formatted blog.

One important tip: If you feared that the more detailed "Articles List," to which you had grown accustomed while reading periodicals on the Kindle 1, has disappeared on the Kindle 2, we bear good news. The Articles List is still there on the Kindle 2, but it's slightly hidden.

While reading any periodical, select the "Sections List" by clicking down on the 5-way. When the Sections List appears on your display screen, use the 5-way cursor to click down on the number in parentheses to the right of any individual section, which represents the number of individual articles in that section. The Articles List for that section will appear on your screen. From the Articles List you can navigate to a specific article by clicking on its headline or you can return to the Sections List by using the 5-way to move the cursor to "Close Articles List" at the bottom of the display and clicking down on it.

Improved Navigation with the 5-Way And the Back Button

Whenever you use the 5-way to "hover" over a hyperlinked word or phrase in your Kindle content, the familiar "hand" icon will appear there on your display. For instance, if you hover almost any underlined words in the Kindle edition of this book, you should see the hand icon, and you can go to the beginning of the Table of Contents by pressing the 5-way. Have you then lost your place? No, just press the "Back" button on the right edge of your Kindle 2 and you will return to this page, or whatever page you were reading from. (I know, it's not exactly a "page," but old habits die hard).

Zoom in to Enlarge Graphics, Tables, and Pictures

The "zoom" feature that was rolled out in a Kindle 1 firmware upgrade just before the launch of the Kindle 2 is much more valuable when combined with the Kindle 2's 5-way. Before that firmware upgrade, the Kindle 1 was pretty useless with most diagrams, charts, and tables. Now, with the Kindle 2 5-way, you simply hover it over any table, map or graphic and you'll see the "magnifying glass" icon that is often associated with a zoom feature. Click on it to enlarge the graphic or, when appropriate, a rotated landscape view on your Kindle display.

One of my favorite uses of this much-improved feature involves enjoying each week's feast of *New Yorker* cartoons. When I first learned that *The New Yorker* would be available for Kindle owners, my first thought was, "Well, fine, but what good is *The New Yorker* if you can't see the cartoons?" With the crisp, clear 16-shade display and the zoom feature, the Kindle 2 resizes each cartoon to the optimal horizontal or vertical fit and lets you browse through them in one "section." That means I can replicate my old habit of thumbing through each issue when it first arrives to enjoy the cartoons.

Instant Onscreen Dictionary Lookup

With the new 5-way it's a snap to look up a word in your Kindle dictionary. Click on any specific word in any form of Kindle content that you can access from the Home screen, and a definition will show up instantly at the bottom your screen.

One of the pleasures of reading any Kindle-formatted document with your Kindle 2 or Kindle DX is that you can use the 5-way to move the cursor alongside nearly word and the Kindle will display, at the bottom of its screen, a thumbnail definition of that word from your on-board dictionary. (The Kindle's default dictionary is the *The New Oxford American Dictionary*, with over 250,000 instant definitions at your disposal). This has become such a routine part of my reading behavior that I've occasionally noticed myself tapping on a word in a print-on-paper book or periodical to see how it's defined. (I'm not sure if this works with print-on-paper reading, but if it does it is very, very, very slow).

But if you're a little frustrated by the tiny font and the often attenuated definition at the bottom of the screen, you can easily view the full definition with all the delights of derivation and usage, in your preferred font size. Just press the Return key on your Kindle's keyboard after a definition appears at the bottom of your screen. You can return instantly to the page you were reading, of course, by pressing the "Back" button on the right edge of your Kindle 2.

The Kindle 2 also makes it easy to choose another dictionary if you prefer it to the *New Oxford American Dictionary*. Simply purchase another dictionary from the Kindle Store, press the Home button on the right edge of the Kindle 2 and then press the Menu button further down the right edge in order to select the Home Screen Menu. From the Home Screen Menu, use the 5-way to underline the "Change Primary Dictionary" option, move the 5-way to underline the dictionary of your choice from your Kindle items listed on the Home Screen, and push the 5-way to select it. (Please note: This feature will not become "live" on your Kindle unless and until you purchase at least one dictionary in addition to the New Oxford American Dictionary that comes installed on your Kindle at delivery. The most popular alternative to this default dictionary is Merriam-Webster's Pocket Dictionary, which is reasonably affordable at a current Kindle Store price of $5.95.

WhisperSync Feature Allows Instant Synchronization of Catalog and Reading Place Across Kindles and Other Devices

Just before launching the Kindle 2, Amazon rolled out a new Kindle Whispersync feature that allows you to synchronize bookmarks and "furthest page read" among multiple Kindles and other Kindle-enabled smartphones and mobile devices. These Kindles and/or other devices must all be registered to the same Kindle account via Amazon's Manage Your Kindle page.

Don't go looking for a Whispersync button on your Kindle 2 hardware or display. Your Kindle 2 arrives with Whispersync turned on, whether or not you own multiple Kindle-enabled devices. If you wish to turn Whispersync off, you should go to Amazon's Manage Your Kindle page (make sure that you're signed in under your own Amazon account, and that this is the account to which your Kindle is registered. Scroll down all the way to the bottom of the page, and you'll see "Manage synchronization between devices. Learn more." Select "Learn more," and choose "Turn synchronization off" to disable Whispersync. If Whispersync is turned off, you can synchronize your Kindles manually to keep your place within a particular book by pressing the "Menu" button on the right edge of the Kindle 2 and selecting "Sync to furthest page read."

While naturally it's nice to be able to synchronize your place among multiple Kindles, there are two very specific ways in which this Whispersync feature will be useful for Kindle 2 owners reading this book:

* First, if you already own a first-generation Kindle and you want to make sure that your Kindle titles are available on and synchronized with your Kindle 2 when it arrives, Whispersync takes care of the migration and synchronization. Just leave Whispersync turned on and you should be all set.

* Second, Amazon and other developers are gradually rolling out features and apps to enable Kindle compatibility on "a range of other devices" such as the iPhone and iPod Touch, other smartphones, netbooks, and other mobile devices. The first of these applications came in the form of the Kindle for iPhone app in March 2009, with features and Kindle Store compatibility that are explained and illuminated by my book, No Kindle Required: The Complete "Kindle for iPhone" User's Guide.

While many Kindle owners will be pleased with their ability to share and synchronize content across multiple Kindles and, eventually, other devices, there are limitations. Some are obvious: Amazon makes it clear in a variety of places that the maximum number of Kindles that can be associated with a single Amazon account, for these purposes, is six. These can include any combination of Kindle 1 and Kindle 2 units. For the large and well-stocked Kindle household, Kindle content obviously comes cheaper by the half-dozen.

What Amazon has yet to tell us is whether that six-unit limitation will also apply to the aggregate total of Kindles and other Kindle-compatible devices once Amazon follows through on its promise to allow other smartphones and mobile devices to read Kindle content. While it may seem logical for Amazon to increase the single-account limit to accommodate, say, six Kindles and six other mobile devices, it's also possible that Amazon will want to tread lightly with publishers on this issue. We've already seen, with the text-to-speech controversy that followed the February Kindle 2 launch, both that some authors and publishers get anxious in a hurry about any perception that the Kindle platform may water down their rights and that Amazon may often be inclined to "go along to get along" to avoid alarming this important business constituency.

Meanwhile, for many Kindle edition titles that are published without Digital Rights Management restrictions via Amazon's Digital Text Platform for indie and other Kindle content publishers, Amazon has removed all limitations on the number of devices on which a customer can download, read, and synchronize ebooks. Many of Amazon's Kindle Store listings now display a line in their Product Details sections that says:

Simultaneous Device Usage: Unlimited

Slightly Improved Content Management and Sorting

Although Amazon has fallen significantly short of fulfilling Kindle owners' hopes for user-defined folders or Gmail-style labeling to help manage Kindle content, there has been a half-measure of improvement in content management functionality.

With the Kindle 1, all content was commingled together so that, frankly, the more you had on your Kindle, the less likely you'd be able to find what you wanted to read with any efficiency.

On the Kindle 2, the combination of some sorting options and the functionality of the 5-way does make it easier to find specific items. To get the feel of these processes, start very simply by pressing the Home button on the right edge of your Kindle. No matter where you are or what you are doing with your Kindle, this will always take you to the device's central Home Screen. The default view for the Home Screen will always be to show you all the items currently aboard your Kindle in a "most recently viewed first" order.

You can easily change this sequence to sort your content by title or by author, or go back to "most recently viewed first," at any time. Just use the 5-way to select from the "Sort options" menu in the upper right corner of the display, immediately below the battery power and wireless connection indicators.

Another equally useful way to get a better look at the specific content on your Kindle involves the "Show options" choices available for your selection in the upper left corner of the display, immediately below your Kindle's "name." Here you can use the 5-way to choose options from among the following:

> All My Items
> Books
> Subscriptions *(which will show you your newspapers, magazines, and blogs)*
> Personal Docs *(which will show you the material that you have converted and transferred to your Kindle via your Kindle.com email address).*

You may also notice that your Kindle 2's Home Screen now automatically aggregates certain content with listings such as "Archived Items," "My Clippings," "Jeff's pictures," and "Periodicals: Back Issues." When you select "Archived Items," you'll see a listing of previously purchased items that you have deleted from your Kindle. Amazon keeps all such titles "in storage" for you, and you can re-download these items to your Kindle wirelessly at any time. The display listing of your books will generally show titles on the left of each line and authors on the right, whereas periodicals will show issue date on the right where you would otherwise expect to see the author's name. Personal documents that come to your Kindle via your kindle.com email address will show your email address on the right.

The Home Screen listings feature a progress indicator in the form of a linear graphic representing where you are in a particular book or other file, and use designations such as "New" if you have yet to open a title or "Sample" if you have downloaded a sample but not the full text. The "New" label will be removed 24 hours after you download an item to your Kindle, but the progress indicator line will still be blank until you begin reading. So before you try to impress your friend or partner by flashing your Kindle to show that you are reading War and Peace, you may want to make sure that the progress indicator doesn't betray an unread book.

Once you have more than a page or two of title listings on your Kindle home screen, you will probably join me in hoping that Amazon eventually comes to understand the importance of providing user-defined folders or labels. Until then, here are a few navigational tips that will employ your intuitive sense of where your various content items will fall in whatever number of pages is occupied by your Home Screen item display:

* When the Home Screen is sorted in "Most Recent First," you can jump to any page in the Home Screen display by using the keyboard to type in its page number.

* Typing in a number higher than the value for the last page will take you to the last page.

* When the Home Screen is sorted in Alphabetical Order by Title or Author, typing in a single letter will take you to the page which contains the first title or author beginning with that letter.

In the same search, typing in two letters in quick succession will take you to the page that contains the first title or author, if any, beginning with those two letters.

You may also want to explore the content management efficiencies that can come with archiving or offloading as much as possible of your Kindle 2 content using the Kindle's seamless new archiving and restoration features. As a Kindle owner, you have access to as much archiving or storage "space" on Amazon's servers as you will ever need for the backup of all the content that you purchase in the Kindle Store.

You can remove any such item from your Kindle and from your Home Screen easily by selecting the item on the Home

Screen, then moving the 5-way to the left and clicking on "Remove from device." The item will then be stored in your Kindle Archives and you can restore it quickly and easily by going to your "Archived Items", a listing which appears at the end of your Home Screen listings, clicking on it to open, finding the item in question by search or browse, and then moving the 5-way to the right to select "add to home." Amazon has greatly improved the ability of Kindle owners to move titles back and forth between their archives and their home screens easily, right from the Kindle 2 home screen. In my case, I'm able to archive about 200 Kindle titles so that my home screen is only about 5 pages long, and thus much more manageable.

Important Note: Titles that you acquire from sources other than the Kindle Store generally cannot be archived on Amazon's servers. If you begin the above archiving/deletion process with, for instance, a title that you have acquired through Mobiguide or Feedbooks, you will see a "Delete this item" message rather than the "Remove from device" message referenced above. Once you delete such a title, it will be gone from your Kindle. Of course, these titles are generally free and should be available for restoration from the same source that you used to acquire them in the first place.

Opening, Deleting, and Restoring Kindle Content

The Kindle 2 provides an easy, seamless process for opening, deleting, and restoring items that you purchase from the Kindle Store. Please be aware that personal documents that you send to your Kindle email address, and other items that you acquire without purchasing them through the Kindle Store, cannot be restored by using the restoration process below.

You can open any item on your Home Screen by going to it with the 5-way and pressing the 5-way to open it.

You can delete any item from your Home Screen (and thus from your Kindle) by going to it with the 5-way and moving the 5-way to the left, then pressing it, to delete the item and remove it from your Kindle.

Fortunately, just in case you delete something by mistake, it is now just as easy to restore previously deleted content back to your Kindle. Just follow the steps in the last paragraph of the previous section.

An Electronic Paper, e-Ink Display Screen, Purpose-Built for Long-Form Reading and Easier Navigation

While we focused some in the previous chapter on the specific hardware enhancements that make the Kindle 2 display easier on the eyes than the screen on the original Kindle, our emphasis here is on the fact that a combination of circumstances now work together to make the Kindle 2 display the most reading-friendly medium invented, since, you guessed it the book itself. A smartphone may be great for text messages, stock quotes, sports results, or weather reports, but if you want to read anything longer than 20 pages, you're going to want either the book itself or the Kindle 2. Case closed. Anyone who tells you he reads novels or the latest book by Thomas Friedman or Sara Lawrence-Lightfoot on an iPhone or a Blackberry is either long on Apple stock or some kind of, er, Android.

The original Kindle certainly aspired to be a device that would disappear as readers dove into the content of their books, but there were too many glitches that got in the way: accidental page-turns, the longer refresh of pages, the inscrutability of charts and graphics without crisp resolution or a zoom feature, the lack of seamless navigation, and so forth. The Kindle 2, with the improvements to display and navigational hardware and menus, nails the reading experience.

III. The Best Features
From the Original Kindle, Improved

Whispernet Wireless Connectivity:
The Kindle's Connection To Millions of Books

The service that Amazon calls Whispernet is actually a 3G EVDO wireless broadband service that enables the Kindle to connect to Sprint's U.S. wireless data network. This service, the same on the Kindle 2 as on the original Kindle, is available in most densely populated areas, but not everywhere. If your Kindle is within Sprint's U.S. wireless data network, you won't need a WiFi connection, a computer connection, or any synchronization steps. The process of ordering a book from the Kindle Store and then seeing it on your Kindle display is only slightly slower than the speed of thought. Of course, if you're outside the network coverage area, the Kindle also comes with a USB cable for easy connection to your desktop or laptop computer. You always have the option of having Amazon send any Kindle content to your computer so that you can transfer it to your computer via USB cable.

When the original Kindle was launched in November 2007, the device's Whispernet-enabled "Basic Web" feature was designated as "experimental," which meant that it could be discontinued by Amazon at any time. There was considerable speculation on Kindle owners' message boards and elsewhere that the web connectivity would eventually be considered too expensive by Amazon and discontinued. However, the service is a popular feature with many Kindle owners, whether one considers it ancillary or essential to the device's connectivity with the Kindle Store, which is the key commercial portal, of course, through which the Kindle and Kindle 2 connect our wallets and credit cards to Amazon's corporate bank accounts. And from our point of view as readers and book buyers, it is the portal through which Amazon is able to dazzle us with nearly instantaneous delivery of the books and other content that we want to read on our Kindles.

Although the Kindle has been marketed initially as an "ebook reader," its array of features actually sets the bar considerably higher than any of its predecessors. Electronic reading devices have been around for decades, but until the launch of the Kindle they failed to gain any serious traction.

These ancillary Kindle features include audio, graphic, and even game-playing capacities, but foremost among them is the Kindle's free broadband wireless connectivity (via the Sprint 3G EV-DO service), which has significant benefits for the device's functionality both with ebooks and with other content. Such a data connection ordinarily costs over $50 to $75 per month, but Amazon pays the entire bill (whatever it is), handles any problems with Sprint, and uses the connection to run a "Whispernet" service that allows Kindle owners to download content – books, newspapers, magazines, and blogs – within seconds of purchasing it from the Kindle Store.

When your Kindle 2 arrives from Amazon, Whispernet will be turned on. In order to turn it off, or turn it back on, press the Kindle 2 "Menu" button on the right edge of the device, position the 5-way to underline "Turn Wireless On/Off," and press down on the 5-way.

Instant Access to a Growing Amazon Catalog

In addition to this wireless connectivity and the Kindle Store's nearly instantaneous content delivery, of course, the Kindle's viability as a reading device owes a great deal to the fact that it is manufactured and sold by Amazon. Over the 13 years prior to its launch of the Kindle, Amazon built enormous brand power among book buyers and book publishers, with over 50 million visitors each month (the lion's share of whom still think of Amazon as a bookseller despite its relentlessly expanding product mix), a catalog of over 4 million book titles, and business relationships with thousands of publishers and authors.

What does this marketplace power mean for the future of the Kindle?

The tens of millions of readers who visit the main Amazon store to find books and other items each month are invariably shown enticing text and graphics about the Kindle. The installed base of Kindle users is approaching 3 per cent of all Amazon customers as I write these words, and will likely reach 4 per cent by the end of 2009 and 6% in 2010. To speculate that it won't keep growing steadily through the next decade would be to assume that the technology, marketing, and marketplace muscle that have brought the Kindle this far will somehow slow to near-stasis. This is not likely.

The thousands of publishers who do business with Amazon, from Random House down to self-published authors with a single title, are regularly invited to make their content available in Kindle editions. Amazon's goal for the Kindle catalog is that it will ultimately give readers access to "every book ever printed." Although large and small publishers have some history of complaint about Amazon tactics and revenue splits, they also have a clear history of nearly universal participation in Amazon's bookselling opportunities. No serious business enterprise can afford to leave the amounts of money represented by Amazon's growing market share on the table.

And for Kindle owners who search for titles that aren't yet available in Kindle editions, Amazon now provides a handy little above-the-fold widget, complete with a miniature picture of a Kindle, allowing a single click to "Please tell the publisher: I'd like to read this book on Kindle."

It may take some imagination and a stunning upward curve to plot progress from the Kindle Store's initial, rather plodding title growth (88,000 titles at launch up to 160,000 titles in August 2008 and over 350,000 titles by September 2009) to the aforementioned "every book ever printed" standard. However, Amazon also has access to the cash and stock shares that it might need to make any deals necessary to buy into other ventures such as the Open Content Alliance and Google Books to digitalize "every book ever printed." Even if such efforts currently seem at odds with Amazon's Digital Rights Management and revenue structures for the Kindle, these boundaries, alliances, and oppositions have a way of changing as technologies change.

No other ebook manufacturer, handheld device manufacturer, or content digitizer has anything like these powers that Amazon possesses. Amazon's marketplace muscle more than offset the Kindle's first-generation flaws, and early indications are that the Kindle's initial success is causing significant loss of market share and traction for relatively worthy competitors such as Sony's e-Reader. At the same time, the prospect that Amazon may soon open the Kindle Store's big tent to other manufacturers' smartphones and other mobile devices may be a significant part of the impetus driving the proliferation of "competing" e-readers coming to market.

Greatly Improved Wireless Web Access

Although Amazon has continued to designate basic web access as experimental on the Kindle 2, features and navigational seamlessness have been added to the Kindle 2's software and documentation so that web access is now much more integral to the Kindle 2 feature set than it was with the original Kindle. Instead of navigating, as it's still possible to do, through the Kindle 2 "Experimental" page to reach the web, a Kindle owner can get to the web and specific web pages in much the same way that works for billions of desktop and notebook computers users every day: start typing a word or phrase with the Kindle keyboard and use the 5-way to click on "google" or "wikipedia" from the search box that will appear instantly at the bottom of the Kindle display screen. Yes, Google is now integral to the Kindle. Stay tuned for a growing, and perhaps major, Amazon-Google partnership.

One important tip for using most of the web features that you'll find in this book: many of them depend upon you changing two settings on the "Basic Web Settings" display screen on your Kindle 2. To reach the "Basic Web Settings" display screen, press the "Menu" button while you are in the Kindle 2 web browser mode, and select "Settings" with the 5-way. When you arrive at the Settings page, make sure that your Kindle 2 is set to "Advanced Mode" on the top line of this screen, and to "Enable Javascript." If you don't anticipate using images as you make use of the Kindle 2 web browser, you can speed up its capacity to process content by selecting "Disable Images" on the bottom line of this display screen.

Since these settings are all "toggle" settings, a hasty look at this web settings screen can be a bit confusing. When you conform your Kindle 2 web browser to the settings I've just described, your screen web settings screen will read as follows from top to bottom:

Settings
Switch to Basic Mode
Clear Cache
Clear History
Clear Cookies
Disable Javascript
Always disabled in Basic Mode
Enable images

Emailing Content to Your Kindle Address

As I became more and more comfortable reading books, newspapers, and magazines on the Kindle, I realized that the Kindle's easy-on-the-eyes fonts and all-in-one-place portability had made it my favorite way of reading just about anything, including memoranda, manuscripts, and even lists of tasks, workout schedules, and recipes. Happily, Amazon provides your Kindle with its own email address and uses that address to send you any files that you send to Amazon for conversion into Kindle-friendly files. (You first have to approve your transmitting email address from your computer, using the "Manage Your Kindle" page on your Amazon account page.) This feature has been retained on the Kindle 2, and because of the new device's enhancements, works even better.

Amazon initially announced that it would charge 10 cents per document to email you these Kindle-compatible files, but appears never to have charged anyone the dime and, at least for now, has dropped the charge entirely. Amazon will convert any document you send in Word, PRC, PDF, HTML, TXT, JPEG, GIF, PNG or BMP format. Just to be clear, that means you can download the complete file of Moby Dick from Project Gutenberg, send it to your Kindle email account that Amazon has provided, and Amazon will zap it to you as a Kindle document at no charge. (If you are out of wireless range – outside the Kindle 2 wireless coverage area or outside the country, for instance – you can also send the document to a slightly different form of your Kindle email address [johndoe@free.kindle.com rather than johndoe@kindle.com] and Amazon will send it to your PC so that you can use your USB cable to transfer it to your Kindle).

You can also receive documents that others email to your kindle.com address, but only if you go to your Manage Your Kindle page on your Amazon account and approve the sender's email address in advance.

Part Three:
Up and Running: Getting Started with Your Amazon Kindle 2

I. Kindle Basics

Charging Your Kindle 2

The first thing to do when you remove your Kindle 2 from the box is to fully charge its battery. Sorry, I know you want to start reading *Ulysses*, but first things first. A full charge on the front end will get you a healthier Kindle and more quality reading time down the road.

Give your Kindle 2 its first charge directly from an electrical outlet by plugging its USB cable into its power adapter, both of which are included in the box, and then plugging the power adapter into an electrical outlet. Later, you'll be able to recharge the Kindle 2 battery simply by plugging the USB into a standard, contemporary USB port on a desktop or notebook computer. The Kindle 2's port for the USB cable is on the bottom edge of the device, right next to the charge indicator light.

When you see a yellow or amber charge indicator light, it indicates that your Kindle 2 battery is charging. You can use the Kindle during this process. (Later, if you charge the battery by connecting your Kindle to a USB port, the Kindle will go into USB mode and you won't be able to use it for reading. However, during this USB charging time you'll be able to perform Kindle content organizing tasks through your computer's "Finder" or "My Computer" pages.)

The charge indicator light will turn green when the Kindle 2 battery is fully charged. Power on your Kindle 2 by sliding and releasing the power switch on the top edge of the Kindle 2, next to the headphone jack.

Registering Your Kindle 2

Your Kindle 2 will already be fully registered when it arrives from Amazon if you purchased it yourself through your Amazon account. However, if you received it as a gift, you can register your Kindle quickly and easily over its Whispernet free wireless service with a computer. Just press the Home and Menu buttons, consecutively, on the right edge of the Kindle 2. Use the 5-way to select "Settings" and, then, to select "Register."

A "Register Your Kindle" dialogue box will appear on your display screen. Enter your Amazon account email address and password, then use the 5-way to select "Submit," and your registration is complete. You can exit this page by pressing the Home button.

You can also register your Kindle on your computer by visiting your Amazon account's Manage Your Kindle page. You'll just need to supply your new Kindle's serial number.

Kindle Repair, Replacement, and Warranties

If, for any reason, your Kindle stops working as you expect it to work, get in touch directly with Kindle Support immediately. You can reach Kindle Support toll-free at 1-866-321-8851 or visit the Kindle Support web page at http://bit.ly/KindleSupport.

Amazon's overall track record in providing customer support to back up its various Kindle models has been excellent. Amazon has shown a willingness to replace individual Kindles with mechanical defects very promptly, with little hassle, and with few questions asked. Early shipments of the Kindle 2 were marred by display issues involving poor contrast and fading in bright sunlight, but in every case of which I was aware, a call to Kindle Customer Support at 1-866-321-8851 led witgh minimal hassle to prompt, free shipment of a replacement unit.

The Kindle comes with a one-year manufacturer warranty that covers such a replacement, but Amazon also sells a two-year extended warranty for the Kindle 2, for $65. But an even better deal, from the leading provider of independent warranties of electronic devices, is SquareTrade's **3-year** warranty on the Kindle 2, for just $34.99. When your warranty is processed, SquareTrade also allows you to add optional accident and spills coverage for an additional $10.

Putting Your Kindle to Sleep and Waking It Up

Whenever you finish reading or otherwise using your Kindle 2, you can extend its battery life and lock out input so that you don't inadvertently enter commands with keys or buttons by putting it to sleep. To put the Kindle 2 to sleep, just slide and release the power button located on the top edge of the Kindle 2. You can then wake it up with the same slide and release of the power button. A screen saver image will appear on the Kindle 2 display when the device is asleep.

Turning Your Kindle Off and On

To completely power down your Kindle 2, just slide the power button located on the top edge of the Kindle 2 and hold it for four seconds before releasing it. To turn it back on, just slide and release the power button without holding it in the slide position.

Choosing Among Six Font Sizes

The Kindle can vastly improve the reading experience for those of us who are challenged by small font sizes. Just tap the "Aa" key at the right of the keyboard's spacebar and you'll be shown an array of six font sizes (as well as commands for the Read-to-Me feature). Just use the 5-way to select the font size that's right for you. This feature generally works in Kindle books, documents, and on the web, but won't work with the Home screen,

screen shots, graphic representations of text, Kindle menus or settings pages, or pages in the Kindle Store.

Although this can vary somewhat based on formatting embedded by a publisher, the six font sizes correspond to type fonts that are 7, 9, 11, 14, 17 and 20-point. This can make a significant difference in your reading ease as most print-on-paper books use fonts that are in the 10-to-12-point range.

Tip: Using a larger font size while you're working on the web or checking your email can be helpful by making it easier to keep hyperlinks separate.

Tip: Using a smaller font size when you're working with clippings or annotations can allow you to capture more text.

Changing the "Leading" Between Text Lines on the Kindle 2

One minor new Kindle 2 feature that may also enhance your reading experience allows you to change the "leading" or uniform space between text lines while you're reading any document. The keyboard command for this feature involves holding down the ALT+SHIFT keys and pressing a number from the number row. The higher the number (between 1 and 9), the wider the spacing between lines. If you try the command now by pressing ALT+SHIFT and pressing 1, you'll see that the leading or spacing narrows so that more lines of text fit onto each display "page," although the text does not change size.

The Care and Feeding Of Your Kindle 2 Battery

Among the numerous features that make the Kindle a "green" device is the fact that its battery has great staying power, requires precious little electricity to recharge and can even be recharged through connecting it to a computer's USB port. You can check battery status as well as your Whispernet signal strength with the indicators in the upper right-hand corner of the Kindle's display screen. (When the Kindle is recharging, the battery strength indicator will be replaced with a little "lightning bolt" graphic.)

Recharging a Kindle's battery via the power adapter is a relatively quick process that usually requires less than two hours. Two recommendations that seem to work for many Kindle owners are (1) recharge your Kindle at the same time each day or evening so that it becomes a regular routine and you always begin the day with a fully charged device; and (2) except when you're traveling, always recharge your Kindle in the same outlet and keep the power adapter near that outlet so that you'll be less likely to misplace it.

The Kindle comes with an AC cord to recharge its battery directly from a conventional U.S. power outlet. Charge the battery up when you first get your Kindle, and generally it should give you back something close to Amazon's claims of four-day battery life when the wireless switch is "on" and up to two weeks of battery life when the wireless switch is "off."

Obviously, the most important thing you can do to save your battery life is to keep the wireless switch "off" when you aren't using the wireless. It only takes a few seconds to connect when you switch it back on.

Updating the Latest Version of Your Kindle's Operating Software

Some of the changes and updates that Amazon will provide for the Kindle 2 in the future will come in the form of firmware updates that will be sent wirelessly to your Kindle via the Whispernet. Two of these updates occurred for the original Kindle prior to the Kindle 2's launch, and for many Kindle owners the updates occurred quietly before they even knew to watch for it.

If you have any concerns about whether your Kindle 2 is running the most up-to-date version of the Kindle system software, it's easy to check. From the Kindle's Home screen, use the Menu button on the right edge of your Kindle 2 to to open the "Menu" screen and select "Settings." The "Settings" page will show you your Account Name, your Kindle's Registration status, Device Name, Kindle email address, and any other Personal Info that you have entered (presumably for the purpose of recovering your Kindle should it be lost or stolen).

Also, at the bottom, of the "Settings" screen, you'll find the "Version" of the software that your Kindle is running. Once you've found this information, use your computer to visit Amazon's "Updating Your Kindle Software" support page. When you scroll down this page you should find the heading called "Verifying Your Software Version," where the version information for Kindle 2 models should match what's displayed at the bottom of your Settings screen on your Kindle 2. If these don't match (and you're certain that you're looking at Kindle 2 rather than first-generation Kindle information), you probably need an update.

If your Kindle's operating software version needs to be updated, this same Amazon support page includes instructions for triggering an update manually, either wirelessly or via USB cable. If you have any difficulty carrying out these instructions, call Amazon immediately at 1-866-321-8851 (inside the U.S.) or 1-206-266-0927 (outside the U.S.).

How to Get Help with Your Kindle

In addition to using this book and the Kindle User's Guide, you will find plenty of helpful information on the Kindle Support website.

You can also call the Kindle Support phone numbers at 1-866-321-8851 (inside the U.S.) or 1-206-266-0927 (outside the U.S.). Telephone customer service staff are available to provide support Monday through Friday from 6 a.m. to 8 p.m. Pacific time and weekends from 6 a.m. to 5 p.m. Pacific time.

If you wish to leave feedback or customer suggestions about the Kindle, send an email to to kindle-feedback@amazon.com.

I also strongly recommend that you visit A Kindle Home Page and use the form near the top of the page to sign up for my free weekly Kindle Nation newsletter. I'm dedicated to making the newsletter a great place to find out about the latest features, enhancements, and "hacks" to add to the many pleasures of using the Kindle, while keeping you up to date on free books and other free content and much, much more.

The newsletter will be delivered to your inbox in a simple format each week, usually with only 4 or 5 small graphics. Please set your email account to allow email messages and to display images from kindlenation@gmail.com. I use a great, extremely safe and seamless service called Constant Contact to manage the Kindle Nation list so that it should always be easy for you to subscribe, unsubscribe, or change your profile details in a snap, and I highly recommend it.

(**Please note**: When signing up for the newsletter, please use your "regular" email address, not the you@kindle.com email address that you would use to send material to your own Kindle. You may, however, feel free to save the newsletter and email it to your Kindle yourself.)

If you want to contact me about pleasures or problems you're experiencing with your Kindle, new ideas you'd like to share, or any other matter concerning this book, send an email to kindlenation@gmail.com. All I ask is that you be aware that I'm an independent author working without a customer service staff, and understand if I sometimes require a few days to keep up with my emails.

Setting Up Your Amazon Account for Your Kindle

Before shopping for or with your Kindle, you may want to streamline the experience in advance by going into "Your Amazon Account" to make sure that your payment information and 1-click purchase settings are correct and up-to-date. If you allow it, the Kindle Store will routinely use your Amazon account's 1-click settings to charge your credit or debit card. If you apply a gift certificate or gift card to your account via your computer, any remaining balance on such an account will be charged for your Kindle purchases before your credit or debit card is charged, but the Kindle won't make this information explicit that during the purchase process. You'll be able to confirm it in your order confirmation email after the fact.

Page Navigation on Your Home Screen

While you're on your Kindle "Home" page, type any number and you'll be taken immediately to the corresponding page of your "Home" listings. Provided, of course, that it exists. If you type 0 you'll be taken to the first page, if you type a number greater than the number of your last page, you'll be taken to the last page.

Alphabetic Navigation on Your Home Screen

While you are on a *sorted* (by title or author) Kindle "Home" page, type any letter and you'll be taken immediately to the page on which the first entry beginning with that letter occurs. Provided, of course, that it exists.

Three Ways to Bookmark Any Page

Bookmark any page you're on, within a document, by pressing "ALT+B," or move the 5-way up or down so that it goes into cursor mode and then press down twice quickly on the 5-way. You can also bookmark any page that you're on by pressing the "Menu" button on the right-hand side of the Kindle 2, then moving the 5-way down until "Add a Bookmark" is underlined and pressing the 5-way once to select. (Please note: Bookmarking generally does not work with Kindle periodicals).

When you've successfully bookmarked a page using any of these three measures, a "dog-ear" icon will appear in the upper right corner of the page.

Note: These bookmarks will be saved and may make it possible to navigate more easily within your Kindle content. However, it's important to know that you don't need to use a bookmark to save the place where you left off reading. Any time you leave a Kindle book or other document, the device will remember your place and return you there the next time you open that document.

II. Getting and Reading Books With Your Kindle

Sampling Books for Your Kindle
From the Amazon Kindle Store

First, try out the Kindle's terrific **sampling** feature. Whether you are browsing titles directly from your Kindle or on your computer, the Kindle edition detail page for just about any title in the Kindle Store will show a button on the right that allows you to send a sample chapter or two (usually about 5% of the full text) directly, and pretty much instantly, to your Kindle. What's not to like about that?

Saving Items for Later
In the Amazon Kindle Store

While checking the detail page for any Kindle content item in the Kindle Store directly from your Kindle 2, you now have the option of clicking on a "Save for later" button right below the "Try a sample" button on the right-hand side of the Kindle display. This option allows you to add an item for your "Save for Later" list so that you can check back on it without cluttering your Kindle and its Home Screen with too many samples. (Note: This "Save for Later" option is not, at this writing, a feature of the Kindle Store when you're shopping from a desktop or notebook computer.)

Buying Content for Your Kindle
From the Amazon Kindle Store

While the Kindle opens up a vast world of free content in the form of public domain books, blogs, website content and documents that you and others can share directly via your kindle.com email addresses, most Kindle owners purchase the lion's share of their Kindle reading content from Amazon's Kindle

Store. If you're browsing and shopping on your home, office or mobile computer, just check out the store and you can choose Kindle Books, Kindle Newspapers, Kindle Magazines, Kindle Blogs, Kindle Store and Kindle Accessories easily from the tabs across the top of the screen. You'll also find helpful tab links to Kindle Support and Kindle Discussions, as well as a "Manage Your Kindle" link.

You can also browse and purchase Kindle edition content directly with your Kindle. Although many Kindle owners prefer to make many of their Kindle content purchases from detail pages to which they've grown accustomed, there will also be plenty of times when you may find it convenient to use your Kindle's "Shop in the Kindle Store" menu option to sample content, save an item for later, or make a purchase immediately. When you take this route, you may be amazed by the speed and seamlessness with which Amazon delivers Kindle content to your device within seconds via the Kindle's Whispernet wireless network. There are few forms of instant gratification more stunning than finding out about an interesting new book in a newspaper, magazine, or blog that you're reading on your Kindle, finding the book in the Kindle Store, and being able to receive it and start reading it within seconds.

Tip: Since the Kindle can make book browsing such a pleasure, you may also experience something that happens to me quite frequently: the desire to flag a title for possible future purchase. Naturally, Amazon has made this an easy process, with two alternative approaches available. The first is the Kindle's **sample** feature. The second is a "Save for Later" link that you will find on the right side of each title's detail page on the Kindle. Just click there and the title will be saved under **"Save for Later" Items** accessible from the menu any time you're in the Kindle Store by way of your Kindle.

Tip: You can maintain up to six Kindles on the same Amazon customer account, with the same name and payment information. If you have multiple Kindle accounts you'll be able to share your book purchases, but not your periodical or blog purchases, among these Kindles. Some publishers, however, may place limitations upon the sharing of their content among multiple Kindles associated with the same account. Other publishers, who have published their Kindle Books free of Digital Rights Management, allow you to read their Kindle books on an unlimited number of devices.

III. Traveling with Your Kindle

As you may have heard, the Kindle 2 is only available for sale "officially" in the United States as of this writing in 2009, and certain features such as those that rely directly and exclusively on the Kindle's Whispernet wireless connectivity are only intended to work within the U.S. In spite of these limitations, the Kindle 2 is nonetheless one of the greatest travel accessories ever invented. Please, don't leave home without it.

Instead of carrying heavy bags full of books on your business trip or vacation, the Kindle 2 will allow you to carry over a thousand books with you in a 10.2-ounce package. Your Kindle will provide you with all the reading content that you download to it, but that's not all.

You may also want to bring your laptop computer and your Kindle's USB cable. Connect your Kindle to the laptop, log in to the Internet anywhere in the world, and you'll be able to get your daily newspapers as well as purchase and download new books, articles, blogs, and magazines. (See p. 173 for more details.) Naturally, you'll have to use a credit card with a U.S. address to make all your Kindle content purchases (as with your purchase of the Kindle itself) since some content currently available in the Kindle Store is material for which Amazon owns only the U.S. selling rights, rather than foreign rights.

In the next few pages I offer a few additional tips to enhance your enjoyment of your Kindle and its remarkable functionality when you are on the road.

Using the Kindle to Translate
Foreign or Technical Words and Phrases

Much has been made of the fact that the Kindle, as of this writing, is not yet available outside the United States, and that some of its appealing features – all of those that depend on a wireless connection – are useless when a Kindle owner lives or is traveling outside the United States or, for that matter, in a Sprint wireless dead zone. However, there are a surprising number of ways in which a Kindle can come in handy when you're on the road, and here is another. This one is helpful if you're traveling in a land where you don't speak the native language.

Before your trip to France, for instance, buy a Kindle edition of a good French-English/English-French dictionary and, of course, download it to your Kindle 2. Then, all you have to do to check on a translation is to type the word with your Kindle keyboard. A "search" field will automatically appear on your display screen and you can search for the word in your translation dictionary simply by moving the 5-way to the right to select "Find." Presto, your Kindle will search for the word or phrase, and you don't even have to select or open the French-English/English-French dictionary first. By selecting and clicking on an iteration of the word or phrase that is associated your bilingual dictionary, you should ordinarily be looking at the translation that you need in a second or two.

By using the same principle and the appropriate reference material, of course, the Kindle can also be used to render professional and technical language and terms. As with any search function, your ability to make effective use of the Kindle's translation powers is bound to improve with use and familiarity.

Making the Most of Your Kindle Connections Overseas

There are myriad reasons why you'll want to take your Kindle on your next trip to a foreign land. Before you go, you'll be able to download many of the books that you might otherwise have to lug with you. And while it's true that you probably won't be able to do any more direct wireless downloading during your trip, that need not keep you from making extensive use of your Kindle.

To make the most of your Kindle overseas, bring your Kindle's USB cable, your laptop, and – if you have one – a Blackberry or other smartphone. In each place where you hang your hat, you'll want to find the best internet connection available – for these purposes, "best" means fast, accessible, and cheap or free. Just because a city that you're visiting has a Starbucks or some other well-known Internet café does not mean that's your best source of Internet access. Technology culture blogger Mike Elgan has written of finding that Starbucks in Greece was charging $660 per month for Internet access, only to discover that "right next door is a better coffee joint where a month of WiFi costs you zero." If you're staying somewhere more than a day or two, a little research to find the "best" connection available should be well worth the time. To find Internet coverage while you're traveling inside or outside the U.S., www.jiwire.com is a helpful resource.

With a daily downloading blast to your computer followed by a USB transfer to your Kindle, you'll easily be able to use your Kindle to keep up with books, newspaper and magazine subscriptions, blogs and other content and read them offline at your leisure during your trip. Just log in to your Amazon account and have your content sent to your computer via the Internet. If you need to receive documents, manuscripts, memoranda, or PDF files while you are abroad, have them sent to your your.address@kindle.com email address and you can transfer them to your Kindle each morning (or any other time of day) with ease.

In a pinch, if you have a smartphone data plan like the AT&T Unlimited Domestic and International Data Plan, you might even be able to tether your laptop to a Blackberry or other device. The economics of such a solution are compelling. The only problem is that such tethering appears to be outlawed under such a plan.

Using the Kindle as a Travel Guide

Whether you're exploring the wonders of your own city or state or traveling around the world, the Kindle can help you get more out of a travel guide than you ever thought possible. The first step, of course, is to purchase and download the travel guides and reference materials that you want for your trip before you leave.

Once this content is "on board" your Kindle, you can search and retrieve material from it, without any wireless or other connection, simply by using the Kindle's powerful local search feature. Technology culture writer and blogger Mike Elgan wrote recently of using Kindle search to learn everything he needed to know in order to maximize his appreciation and understanding of ancient Greek ruins such as the Temple of Poseidon while en route to the sites.

Once you've got good reference material on your Kindle, all you have to do is begin typing any word or phrase up to 255 characters with your Kindle keyboard. The Kindle 2 will show a search field on the display screen that will allow you to search your onboard content or widen the search to include Google, Wikipedia, or the web. By selecting and clicking on a reference from your travel material, you can be reading up on any topic within a moment or two.

The Kindle and GPS

The first-generation Kindle included a very rudimentary GPS capacity that suggested interesting potential but wasn't very useful because of the Kindle 1's hardware limitations. Rather than enhance Kindle GPS with the Kindle 2 – whose zoom feature and 5-way functionality might actually realize the GPS' potential – Amazon has inexplicably dropped the GPS or hidden it so well that we haven't yet been able to find the keyboard commands to activate it. The Kindle hardware and 3G service make it unlikely that GPS is entirely gone from the Kindle 2, but unless and until Amazon goes "open source" with the Kindle 2 so that developers are able to help unlock some of its unrealized potential, we'll just have to stay tuned.

Downloading Kindle Editions Via USB Cable

Being outside the Kindle's wireless service area, or even outside the U.S., need not be an obstacle to getting Kindle edition books, newspapers and other content quickly, as long as you have a computer with Internet access and an Amazon account, linked to your Kindle, with a U.S. credit card as the registered form of payment. In addition to your Kindle and a connected computer, the other piece of hardware that is essential for this operation, of course, is the USB cable that comes in the box with the Kindle. (Note: This is a device-specific USB cable rather than a cable with standard USB connections at both ends, although I was happy to find during a recent crisis of disorganization that the device-specific USB cable that had come with an old Creative Zen MP3 player a few years back was a perfect fit for the Kindle).

The process is simple and straightforward:

* Just log on to your Amazon account on your computer, go to the title's Kindle Edition detail page, and purchase the book, newspaper, magazine, or blog. (Naturally, it won't show up immediately on your Kindle, since the Kindle is not connected wirelessly via the Whispernet.)

* Your next move, therefore, will be to navigate to the Manage Your Kindle page of your Amazon account, and scroll down to "Your orders and individual charges." You may sort your downloads by title, by author or by purchase date. Then just choose the title you want to download from those you have already purchased, and select "Computer" from the "Download/Send to..." pull-down menu at the right. As the download occurs, make a note of the download location on

your computer so that you'll be able to find the download easily for the next step.

* Once your download has occurred, make sure that your Kindle is in "on" and "awake" mode, and connect your Kindle to your computer via the USB cable. Then just transfer the new Kindle content from your computer to your Kindle. Be sure to place reading content in your Kindle's "documents" folder, Audible.com files (.aa) in the "audible" folder, and other audio content in the music folder.

* Once you have made this transfer, disconnect your Kindle from your computer and – perhaps after a few seconds while you see an "Updating" message at the bottom of the Kindle screen – you'll be able to read the new content on your Kindle.

If the content you wish to transfer to your Kindle is in the form of subscription content for a newspaper, magazine, or blog, you will of course have to repeat this process for each daily, weekly, or monthly transmission of content. With subscription content, it will be helpful to select the "Newspapers" or "Magazines" sorting view that is available on the right side of the screen under "Your orders and individual charges." Be aware that with daily issues of a newspaper, these issues will only be available to you for direct download from Amazon for a period of one week. Once you've downloaded them to your Kindle, you may select certain issues that you wish to keep indefinitely on your Kindle by using the 5-way to move the cursor to the right and choosing "Keep This Issue" from the menu of options that appears on your Kindle screen.

IV. Other Tips and Tricks to Help You Get the Most out of Your Kindle 2

Keep a Picture Album on Your Kindle

This one is fun!

1. Connect your Kindle to your desktop and navigate through "My Computer" to your Kindle. On a PC, the Kindle will probably be recognized as an "E" or "F" drive by your computer, depending on your hardware configuration, whereas a Mac's "Finder" app will call your Kindle a "kindle." When you click on your Kindle to open it you will find that its storage is already configured with 4 folders called Audible, documents, music, and system.

2. Add a new folder called "**pictures**" alongside the three existing folders. Within the new "**pictures**" folder, create a subfolder for any group of pictures you want to be able to browse through. Name these subfolders so that you'll recognize them when they show up on your Home screen's list of titles. Then copy the applicable pictures – they must be formatted as jpg, gif or png – into each folder from your desktop computer. Disconnect your Kindle from your desktop after you've finished copying pictures, and your Kindle should return in a few seconds to your home page. **Important note: You must follow the exact instructions here and call the folder "pictures." If you call it "photos," for example, the Kindle will not recognize it.**

3. From "Home," type "ALT+Z" to prompt your Kindle to recognize the new subfolder as a "Book." Open the "Book" and use "Next Page" and "Previous Page" to browse through your Kindle photo album. Once you've opened the photo album, press the "Menu" button on the right edge of your Kindle 2 for additional options. Several commands on the local menu at the bottom of the screen will allow you to adjust your view. You can also type "F" to set or leave "full screen mode," or use the 5-way to move the cursor

over a picture to bring up the "magnifying glass" icon, then zoom in by pressing down on the 5-way.

4. Although it's essential that you name the primary photo album subdirectory "pictures," you can use other names within that subdirectory to organize your photo album.

Optimizing the Powers of Kindle Search

Like Google Desktop and Google Search, the Kindle has the power to use a single search to probe through your onboard Kindle documents, your onboard dictionary, Wikipedia, Google's web search engine, and the Amazon Kindle Store for all occurrences of any given word, term, or phrase that you provide. From any document that you're reading, just begin typing any word or phrase up to 255 characters on your Kindle 2 keyboard and a search field will appear on the display screen. If you move the 5-way to the right and select "Find," the Kindle 2 will search within that document. If you keep moving the 5-way to the right, past "Find," you will be presented with other self-explanatory options:

> My Items
> Store
> Wikipedia
> Google
> Dictionary

Begin the specified search by moving the 5-way to your choice and pressing down. If you begin your search from the Home Screen, your Kindle 2 will display a larger search box with the five aforementioned choices as well as an additional "Go to Web" option.

The Kindle search process is often a quicker and smoother way to reach specific web destinations than opening the web browser as a separate step from the Kindle home screen. If your wireless switch is in the "off" position, of course, your search will be limited to the document you're reading, the documents that you have downloaded or emailed to your Kindle, and to your onboard dictionary. You can also begin a dictionary search by moving the cursor alongside any word in a document, and a brief definition will appear instantly on your display screen.

One other lesser-known use of the Kindle's search powers is that they allow you to find books and other content without knowing their titles. When I type in "Let us go then you and I" in the search input field of my Kindle and begin a search of "My Items," it will come up with the title *Prufrock and Other Observations*, by T.S. Eliot, which I previously purchased and downloaded to my Kindle, as well as references in Wikipedia and elsewhere on the web.

V. Kindle 2 Shortcuts

In addition to all the shortcuts that you'll find chapter-by-chapter as you proceed through this book, we are isolating a number of convenient shortcuts here that should help you find your way around the world of the Kindle 2 right from the start.

Power Switch Shortcuts

The power switch is located on the top edge of the Kindle 2, to the left of the audio jack. Note that, unlike the Kindle 1, the Kindle 2 wireless does not have an on-off power switch. The wireless feature, which includes your connection to the Kindle Store as well as to Wikipedia, Google, the web, and your kindle.com email service for personal documents, can be turned on and off with a toggle command at the top of any Kindle 2 menu.

Put the Kindle 2 to Sleep: To put the Kindle 2 to sleep, slide the power switch to the right, then release it (it will snap back to the left naturally).

> * The Kindle 2 display will show a screen saver when the device is in Sleep mode.

* If you are using a Kindle 2 audio feature such as "Read-to-Me" or "Play MP3," the audio will continue to play when the device is in Sleep mode.

* The Kindle will also automatically enter Sleep mode if you don't engage it for a few minutes, much as would happen with any other computer.

Awaken or Turn On the Kindle 2: To awaken or turn on the Kindle 2 when it's been off, asleep or reset, slide the power switch to the right, then release it (it will snap back to the left naturally).

* When it's been in the Off or Sleep mode, the Kindle 2 should return the last page or screen that you were on before it powered down or went to sleep.

* When it'as been reset (rebooted), the Kindle 2's blank display should refresh itself several times over the course of a few seconds, then show a graphic representing the re-booting process. When it's ready to use you'll see the Home Screen on the Kindle 2 display. It may, for a few seconds, look as if your Kindle is empty, but this should resolve itself quickly.

Turn the Kindle 2 Off: To turn the Kindle off, slide the power switch to the right and hold it at there for at least four seconds, then release it.

* The Kindle 2 display will show a blank screen when the device is in Off mode.

* If you're using a Kindle 2 audio feature such as "Read-to-Me" or "Play MP3," the audio will cease to play when the device is in Off mode.

* If you notice that your Kindle enters Off mode without your having manually turned it off, it has probably shut down due to loss of battery power. If this occurs, it's best to connect the Kindle to a power source before attempting to turn it on again.

Reset the Kindle 2: Reset or reboot the Kindle 2 by sliding the power switch to the right and holding it at there for at least 15 seconds, then releasing it. The Kindle 2 will fully power down, and its cache(s) will be cleared so that it won't return to the same page you were reading when you turn it on again. Some web information such as the username and password for an email website will need to be entered again.

> * The Kindle 2 display will show a blank screen when the device is in Off mode.

> * If you're using a Kindle 2 audio feature such as "Read-to-Me" or "Play MP3," the audio will cease to play when the device is in Off mode.

> * When you turn it on again by moving the power switch to the right and releasing it, the Kindle 2's blank display should refresh itself several times over the course of a few seconds, then show a graphic representing the rebooting process. When it is ready to use you'll see the Home Screen on the Kindle 2 display.

Menu Tips and Shortcuts

Many of the commands that can be triggered with the Kindle 2 keyboard or 5-way controller can also be accessed from various Kindle 2 menus, and we present a few here to get you started. As you become familiar with these options, you'll develop your own comfort level with finding your best personal choices for getting where you want to go with your Kindle 2.

See the Time: To see the time on your Kindle 2 at any time from any screen, just press the Menu button on the right edge of the Kindle 2. The time that's shown will be based on the address to which your Kindle was shipped. But a little heads up here: be careful! The time that displays at the top of the Menu screen does not automatically refresh every minute, unless you manually go in and out of the Menu display. So if you are dissolving into a great novel and you feel like time is just standing still, sorry, but you better check the Kindle clock again.

Start or Stop the Kindle 2 MP3 Audio Feature: Hold down the ALT key to the left of the space bar and press the space bar.

Advance to the Next Song in the Kindle 2 MP3 Audio Feature: Hold down the ALT key to the left of the space bar and press the letter "F".

Keyboard Shortcuts

Start or Stop the Kindle 2 Text-to-Speech Read-to-Me Feature with SHIFT+SYM: Hold down the SHIFT (Up-Arrow) key and press the SYM key to the far right of the spacebar. You'll find this shortcut is far more convenient than the other means of activating or stopping the Kindle 2 Text-to-Speech Read-to-Me Feature, through the Font (Aa) key menu to the near right of the space bar.

Pause or Resume the Kindle 2 Text-to-Speech Read-to-Me Feature: Just press the space bar. (If you press the space bar and a typing dialog field open up at the bottom of the display screen, it's a good indication that the Kindle 2 Text-to-Speech Read-to-Me Feature is inactive.)

Bookmark Any Page or Website with ALT+B: Hold down the ALT key and press the letter "B". If you're on a page in a book, periodical or other file in regular Kindle 2 reading mode, bookmarking a page will create a tiny darkening-in change in the dog-ear that you see in the upper right-hand corner of that page. The bookmark will then show up in the "My Notes and Marks" listing that you can display from the Menu display for that book or document. (You can also bookmark a page from the Menu display.)

Web Shortcuts

Instead of using the Menu process by starting at the Home screen and choosing Menu>Experimental>Basic Web to get to the web, you can get there more quickly by clicking on one of the links in this book. Even if the link is not a link to precisely where you want to go, you will be on the web and will be able to get to your web bookmarks, web history, a URL entry screen, or the Kindle Store just by pressing the Menu button and making your selection.

Another quick way to the web is to begin typing a search keyword or phrase. A search dialogue field or display box will appear at the bottom of the screen, and you can go directly to the web by moving the 5-way to the right twice and choosing Google or Wikipedia. Finishing the typing of the search term, of course, will get you to a more specific web location, but you will get to the web either way. (As you can see, the search dialogue feature can also initiate a search of the particular book or document you are reading, your onboard Kindle 2 dictionary, your entire library, or the entire Kindle Store.)

Kindle Store Shortcuts

Search an Author's Content in the Kindle Store: Just type @author [author's name] on the search line while you are in the Kindle Store to begin a search for all content in the Kindle Store by that author. You can also initiate a similar search from any reading page by typing @author [author's name] on the search line, moving the 5-way to the right twice, and selecting "store."

INDEX

About the Author

Stephen Windwalker, a pen name, is a Boston native who lives in Arlington, MA. He is the author of several books of fiction and nonfiction, the founder and publisher of the Kindle Nation Blog, and the founder of Harvard Perspectives Press. He cut his teeth as a writer covering the Cape Cod Baseball League while a teenager, but survived to graduate with honors from Harvard College, where he studied the craft of writing with Monroe Engel, Kurt Vonnegut, Robert Lowell and Carter Wilson.